# TOTAL PROPAGANDA

## DUNDURN
### TORONTO

# HELEN RAZER

# TOTAL PROPAGANDA

## BASIC MARXIST BRAINWASHING FOR THE ANGRY AND THE YOUNG

Publisher and acquiring editor: Scott Fraser | Editor: Luke Savage
Cover designer: Sophie Paas-Lang
Cover image: stock.adobe.com/GeorgiosKollidas
Printer: Marquis Book Printing Inc.

**Library and Archives Canada Cataloguing in Publication**

Title: Total propaganda : basic Marxist brainwashing for the angry and the young / Helen Razer.
Names: Razer, Helen, author.
Identifiers: Canadiana (print) 20200268082 | Canadiana (ebook) 20200268120 | ISBN 9781459747739 (softcover) | ISBN 9781459747746 (PDF) | ISBN 9781459747753 (EPUB)
Subjects: LCSH: Socialism—21st century. | LCSH: Socialism and youth. | LCSH: Generation Y. | LCSH: Socialism and society.
Classification: LCC HX547 .R39 2020 | DDC 320.53/15—dc23

We acknowledge the support of the Canada Council for the Arts and the Ontario Arts Council for our publishing program. We also acknowledge the financial support of the Government of Ontario, through the Ontario Book Publishing Tax Credit and Ontario Creates, and the Government of Canada.

Care has been taken to trace the ownership of copyright material used in this book. The author and the publisher welcome any information enabling them to rectify any references or credits in subsequent editions.

The publisher is not responsible for websites or their content unless they are owned by the publisher.

Printed and bound in Canada.

VISIT US AT

 dundurn.com |  @dundurnpress |  dundurnpress |  dundurnpress

Dundurn
3 Church Street, Suite 500
Toronto, Ontario, Canada
M5E 1M2

# 2010-2020
## (Decade of Glorious Worldwide Revolt)

---

## Karl Marx Is A Super Cool "Bro" And Totally Relevant For Today's "Cell Phone" Crazy Youngster!

---

Karl Marx was a white European dude from the nineteenth century who drank too much and probably got the cleaning lady knocked up. He was often in a very bad mood. If we saw him on a TED talk of the present, we might ask, "Can't that crusty old drunk break out a smile once in a while, or possibly a comb?" before switching to another speaker. Perhaps one with tidier hair and a more optimistic topic than This Is How The World Went To Shit.

Such was the unpleasant labor of a sometimes-unpleasant man: exploring the shit of the world in some detail. This short book will not be a guide to the life of Marx, which may or may not have involved a weekend of banging a German cleaning lady called Helene. It will be a basic introduction to the revolutionary project of sorting shit out, begun in earnest by Marx. One that has enjoyed a recent revival.

You may have heard the old term "socialism" going around a bit lately. You *must* have, otherwise you'd hardly have picked up a book that promises to explain Marx's marvelous version of it. I should tell you then, from the outset, that the Marx kind of "socialism," which I'll now stop putting in scare quotes, *is largely a tool for understanding capitalism*. And capitalism is understood by the Marxist to negatively affect many parts of everyday life, not *just* the bits with money in it.

Yes. Not *just* the economy! This news may be a relief for you, because it means we'll discuss things a bit more thrilling than profit, commodities, and labor. We will talk about a world in which we might all flourish. We will even talk about our feelings. Our feelings are not, when truly examined, unimportant when it comes to diagnosing all the disorders of capitalism. And Marx was in the business of diagnosis. It's now up to us to find a cure, a task you may find, as I do, both thrilling and fucking exhausting.

As we've seen over the latter half of the past decade, this socialism word can once again be used loudly and proudly. You may have heard it used by the United States presidential candidate Bernie Sanders during his astonishingly popular campaigns of 2016 and 2020. If you were listening in to the 2017 French Presidential election, you would have heard the word truly and more traditionally used by Jean-Luc Mélenchon. You may have heard it used by the record numbers of young people joining political parties like British Labour or organizations like the Democratic Socialists of America (DSA). You might even have heard it even earlier, had you attended one of the many anti-austerity protests that swept the globe during the first half of the decade following the colossal capitalist clusterfuck that was the 2008–2009 economic crash. If you ever joined me and my family at a table, you would have heard it then, too. As in, there goes the socialist again, going on about seizing the means of production while totally covered in gravy. I am delighted to find a more agreeable place and time than Christmas dinner in which to address the topic.

For various reasons, which you can be sure I will start boring you with in Chapter 1, talk of socialism — which can also be called "communism" by some, or, just to mess with your shit, "the materialist Left" — has lately become more frequent and public. It's not just for the festive family table or nineteenth-century white men anymore! No. Apparently, many inquisitive youngsters of the West have decided they don't mind the sound of this thing at all, this form of socialism written down by Marx in the mean little rooms of a long-ago Europe.

You, whether old or young or a midlife husk like me, have not become curious about something like socialism on a whim. To take real interest in any "ism" is a time-sucking pain, especially when that ism has endured decades of bad press. And it has had *such* bad press. Everyone is always calling someone a "Marxist" as though this is a slur; as though they even understand what Marxism means in an era where it is no longer truly taught at universities.

You might have heard people say that Marxism is too ideal-istic, too lazy, or about as helpful to the present day as a derelict coal mine. Such people — often old enough to remember the Cold War and usually rich enough to own a bit of property — have many ways of dismissing Marx's socialism without ever bothering to read it. These include, "There's no difference between Left and Right anymore. That garbage went in the trash with my iPhone 2."

Well, you know, fuck 'em. If we *truly* understand what Marxism is — a strong and unflinching criticism of capitalism, the neces-sary shadow of a behemoth that imposes itself on every person on the planet, no matter their cultural identity — then plainly, there's a bunch of Western people, largely young, now reasserting their need to do this.

We see many respectable books published about the rise of the "alt-right." We read many news articles profiling young, smug conservatives calling for an end to immigration/feminism/decent manners and we see media vision of groups that advance crude nationalism. What we do not see in mainstream press is the strong re-emergence of great Leftist passion. This is the true shift of our time. Right now across the West, there are rallies and political par-ties full of kids united by one crucial understanding: capitalism cannot be trusted to determine our future.

Look at 'em all! Oh, they warm even my dead old heart. Young people were very recently in very high attendance at rallies for self-described socialist politicians like Sanders, himself often flanked by perhaps the globe's most popular socialist millennial: Congresswoman Alexandra Ocasio-Cortez. Young people answered a range of social surveys in 2016 that showed strong favorability for socialism and strong suspicion of capitalism. In America of all places, that oh-so-capitalist country, polls suggest that roughly half of young adults are basically ready to toss the ruling economic system straight into history's proverbial dustbin. There are babies engaging in some fiery Red criticism of things as they are in the West.

Young people are even beginning to find their way into my inbox. They have been sending emails and Facebook messages, asking, "Old Lady, what is Marxism?" when they have detected reference to Marx in my published writing. I started out telling them what Marxism was *not*: it was *not* placing faith in the power of cautious or "politically correct" words to change reality; *not* thinking that a truly good change in the world will ever be made by those already powerful; *not* worrying so much about whether you are a noble individual, and more about how you can stand shoulder to shoulder with others to win a noble future.

One day, I received a correspondence from a bright young lady called Ana who demanded to know what Marxism *was*, not what it *wasn't*.

I told her a little. Ana told me that such analysis was "lit fam." She assured me, when asked, that this was not an insult, and then requested more information on the man's thinking. I asked her exactly *how* interested in Marx she felt she was, so I knew how much time to spend explaining and/or ripping off ebooks to send her. She said she had read a bit about him and he was "turnt as fuck" — apparently, again, not an insult — and that she would certainly like to read more, if only she, an Uber driver and a writer and a shop assistant, had the free time. Could I sum it all up? So here it is, Ana: the evaporated Marx. The decision to write this book was taken after many queries of the type, but yours was the first, and the rudest.

This book, of course, is not just for time-poor kids surviving that shitstorm we call the "gig economy." It has been written for anyone who wants to taste a little Marxism before committing to feast upon the bodies of the tender ruling class marinated in riches for centuries. (Please note, employees of Rupert Murdoch, this is a *joke*. Neither Marx nor I are advocates for cannibalism. We're just trying to stop capitalism from eating the people.) But, as the young seem to have worked up quite an appetite, I must first tip my Lenin cap to them.

To this end, young comrade, I apologize in advance for being so old. I should warn you that I could not identify a "dank meme" if the fate of the working class depended on it and that I shall not be "shipping" Lenin and Trotsky. If I tried to speak your marvelous language, I would produce sentences like, "Hey, fleeky brother with the random, let's get planked with Marx!"

Nobody wants that. But, what many do seem to want is a short and new explanation of an old and complex thinker. So, this is that revolutionary tapas; an introductory morsel of Marx. Think of it as a tasting plate.

Again, young comrade, I am *sorry* in advance for being me. Ideally, this book would be written by a fashionable person like Ana who does not have to google terms like "woke" — which, I recently learned, is a pretty good one. "Woke" is what a Marxist would call "class consciousness," and more of that later. For the minute, my attention is still with you poor fucking Millennials, the most impoverished Western generation in almost a century.

You guys have it rough. Without extraordinary reform to the way we organize our economies, you lot, as some of you may have started to suspect, are soon going to have it worse. Unless your parents are both generous and extremely well-to-do, the future you face is one of absolute uncertainty. This uncertainty is often rebranded for you by politicians and property owners as your opportunity to be "agile," "innovative," or "entrepreneurial." To which the Marxist says, "Get fucked."

There is nothing character building about not being able to afford a permanent place to live. There is nothing fun about a shrinking job market. Stagnant wages are not exhilarating, and spending a huge sum of money on an education that qualifies you for work that may not even exist by the end of your degree hardly makes this An Exciting Time To Be Alive. The only people truly enjoying themselves in the present are the elite investor class, the people you might have heard called "the one percent" but which we might now more accurately call, and plenty of good economists do, the one percent of the one percent.

You have it bad, comrades. And, no, of course, in anticipation of the "You don't know how good you have it, shut up and enjoy your avocado toast" critique so many young people face, you don't have it as bad as your comrades in the Global South. You're not sleeping in the factory dormitories of China or mining rare elements in the bloody pits of Congo. And, yes, you have nice things like your Uber and your streaming video, and your low-cost creative fashions, all of which you access on devices made by those Chinese and Congolese laborers.

But what you *don't* have, as you may have begun to see, is the future you were promised. You've been told for all your life that You Can Make It If You Try. And perhaps you now see that no amount of trying can secure you a regular job, a home or, in many cases, the means to an education. Even the thought of having your own child must be tempered with thoughts of money. Commandments like "Follow your dreams!" make a lot less sense when capitalism has become your nightmare.

You are *not* a pussy for feeling that the world has failed you. The world *has* failed you, and it's hardly your fault that its systems have begun to break down. You guys are *not* "choosing" to bounce from job to job. You are *not* choosing to hurt those Chinese and Congolese workers who made that iPhone with their blood. You did *not* throw your chance at a home after a gourmet sandwich.

Oh, Millennial Sandwich Eater. The next time a Boomer investor accuses you of eating your asset-rich future in the form of a snack, tell them you would need to sacrifice 16,420 fifteen-dollar sandwiches to save for the median American house price of $246,300. That's almost a half-century of daily sandwich denial, by which time you will be considered too old to service a loan.

You have no "choice" about buying a home — the choice has been made for you by a political economy so self-deluded it can no longer identify its own bad ideas. So, its defenders make up moral bullshit instead. They say to you, a large group of people, "You're only poor because you're spoiled brats." This is a cop-out. It is not "economics." It is *not* an explanation.

Old or young, you may sometimes wonder about the deteriorating conditions of your own life. Rich or poor, you may wonder about the broken lives of others, in neighboring suburbs and distant lands. You might not be able to stand thinking too long about those others. Questions about who made your iPhone, or why the Sudanese guy driving the Uber it beckoned looks so miserable and homesick and scared, are those that are hard to endure.

While a Marxist view might not make these questions any simpler for your heart to take, it can ease the strain to your head. Questions about the origin of the suffering and poverty borne by so many in this present world — in which just eight men command more wealth than the poorest half of the planet, in which one billion go hungry, in which corporations are now excused both from paying tax *and* providing meaningful employment — can be answered, possibly even corrected, by the socialism of Marx.

Marxism is a way of understanding how we got here. Marxism is a way of answering heartbreaking questions. Marxism is … well, we better let that dirty old bastard begin a book that would never have been written without him. Marxism is a criticism of the present that gives rise to a vision for a society in which "The free development of each is the condition for the free development of all."

Now. Let's talk about that freedom, shall we? For each and for all.

# 1

---

## Poor People In History! Who Never Even Had "Flip Phones"! Wow! Were They Poor Because They Were Thinking Negative Thoughts?!

---

Freedom. What a baffling turd of a word. Everybody claims they want it, yet so few have offered powerful descriptions of where it might be, much less how we could recognize it when we found it. What Marx gives us is a map for the modern world's escape to freedom; a map with living creatures drawn in great detail, all wearing history's chains. Chains that are hidden throughout an era, then reveal themselves as that era ends.

Now, Marx wrote down this account of our chains well over a century ago. You might therefore suppose, as many do, that these rusted chains have simply fallen off us, and that we shouldn't be paying any attention to declarations made by some antique beard.

In very unsurprising news, I'm of the view that Marx and his beard have a great deal yet to offer, and this book is an effort to convince you, over and over again, that he still gives us a way to identify our present-day chains — chains that you may already, or soon will, agree have begun to be visible, indicating that this era is drawing to a close. In other words, it can take us decades, or even centuries, to see the things that bind us. This chapter is an effort to explain the Marxist way of seeing how this bondage forms, how our chains take on new forms over time, and how the fuck to get rid of them for good.

So, before I explain *how* Marx's old spyglass works, even before I tell you its name, let's begin to simply *see* it work. Let's look at what many say is the world's most visible "chain" right now. Let's look first — you *knew* it had to happen, so we might as well get it over with — at Trump.

When this monstrous stain spread to the world's most influential office, there were, broadly speaking, three primary reactions from us in the West. One, which we will have little business with here, was, "Great! I hope he shakes things up and gives those politically correct elites a good pussy grabbing." Another was, "What a shame for humanity that Hillary Clinton didn't win." A third was, "Don't make me choose. They both suck."

If this last reaction was yours, then, congratulations, comrade: you're in for a lifetime of arguing with just about everyone you meet. You may also be in for some Marxism. Why? Because you see that politics are not *either* black or white, but sometimes black and white *at once*. Because you see how the conflict between two forces, in this case the politics represented by Trump and those by Clinton, might not be best settled between them, but that a *third* possibility must be synthesized. Because "lesser of two evils" doesn't cut it. Because you see that a guy like Trump is not just a monster, but a monstrous product of history. Because you reject simplicity.

Trump himself appears not to reject simplicity. He embraces it. He is, at least in his public presentations, a simple man. He offers simple, usually ugly, answers to the kinds of questions asked of politicians by the people — mostly, he doesn't even answer at all and just describes himself as *tremendous*. But his tremendously terrible appearance in history is not the simple matter it first appears; in fact, it's so complex we need a mapmaker like Marx to help us plot it out.

Trump's victory, along with the recent rise of hard, racist politics across the West — Hungary, the Netherlands, France, Italy, Germany, the UK, Sweden, and Australia — tells us something. It tells us that liberal democracy, the name we usually give to the kind of government and economy that we in the West have, has begun, quite seriously, to fail. If it were not failing, then people throughout the world, both in its dominant Western economies and in the exploited trade nations of the Global South, would not be having such a shit time. If people did not detect it failing with their senses, then they would not be openly rejecting old solutions, albeit, in the case of voting for Trump and other deluded racists, in a horrific and desperate way.

People committed to choosing the "lesser evil" argue that things aren't shit. They say, "History always gets better!" even when their own senses are telling them the opposite is true. They say, knowing well that the people are starving, that everyone is satisfied with their meal. They have said this to justify the brutal policies of many dictators, including those who pretended to be "communist." They said this in Philadelphia, July 2016.

"Don't let anyone ever tell you that this country isn't great," said the gracious Michelle Obama at the Democratic National Convention, poised and passionate, beautiful and enraged, refuting the claims of the Trump campaign. Trump's "Make America Great Again" slogan that she denounced was, of course, one way of saying things were shit. When FLOTUS said so unequivocally that things *weren't* shit, I began preparing for a world whose most powerful person would be a fuckwit who'd never learned to knot a tie.

But the response by many of my journalist colleagues to this speech was numb awe. They thought Michelle, long considered one of her husband's most effective political assets, had delivered a patriotic knockout blow. This persuasive woman — whom they call "the closer" in DC — had, as far as many were concerned, the best and the last word on Trump.

As things turned out, she hadn't: the fuckwit got elected. If we listen to her speech like Marxists — people who see black and white at once, people who see the forces of history at play — we can begin to detect the reason why. Which is not to say that we would have known for sure, if only we'd listened *hard* enough, that this was a herald of crisis. But it was a pretty loud alarm. A few commentators familiar with Marxist thought publicly sounded it. A few of us on the sidelines said, "That was a bad speech for the party. Mrs. Obama just lost Mrs. Clinton a lot of votes by telling an obvious lie." I said this on Facebook. Twenty people unfriended me. I also had godmother privileges revoked, which I hadn't known was a possible thing.

To say that the Democratic Party failed to admit that the American people live largely in shit is not to say that Trump is a great guy, or even that the Democratic Party is evil. But this is how such statements are generally interpreted by folks who can see only black or only white, and not black and white *both* present in a single instant. An instant, in this case, of immense historical change.

Let's be clear. Trump is a broken toilet, and we wish the old bog plumbing problems. But, his claim that a nation needed improvement was one that even the charismatic Mrs. Obama couldn't counter. She tried to deny the hard reality that many were living, or the one that they reasonably feared. It didn't work. An upbeat lie can make the pain of reality worse. You can't keep telling people that the solution to their problems is believing they don't have any problems. This is best summed up in the completely unrelated words of daytime television's Judge Judy: "Don't pee on my leg and tell me it's raining."

Sixty-three million people had been peed on for so long that they put their faith in a terrible umbrella. And, no, it *doesn't matter* that Hillary won the popular vote. It *doesn't matter* that Trump was never going to make things better. All that matters is that he acknowledged the need for change to happen. *Tens of millions of people* were moved to the polls by that lying turd. That his ideas resonated for so many demands, for the Marxist, a bit more analysis than "People are stupid," or "People are no damn good."

What drives people to vote for such a clockwork banana? Is it just that they're awful, and possibly deeply racist? There's a lot of the latter going on, sure. America is, like all Western nations, a place shaped in part by its loathing for dark skin. But, the loathing for visible otherness tends to become more extreme in certain conditions. And the racist loathing might not even play a part for some: there were counties that had voted for Barack Obama, a brown dude, *twice*, that switched their allegiance in 2016 to this asshole. These voters were unlikely to have all suddenly caught a dose of racism. If they disliked anything, it was the lack of "greatness" in their lives.

America, in the experience of many, did not, and does not, feel "great." Economic decline — one that sees your income drop, your neighbors lose their homes and your town centre shuttered — tends not to be an awesome experience. This is what is happening across the United States of America, a nation that a newly low-income American associate described to me as "a Third World country with great PR."

Michelle Obama's insistence that the United States *was already great* did Clinton, who continued to make the claim, great damage. Someone who works at Walmart, America's largest employer, for eleven bucks an hour can only hear that things are "great" for a limited time. To hear this from Clinton, a nominee who once held an executive position at that low-wage employer, must have been particularly galling. Eventually, long work hours, low pay and the fact that, following the real estate–led financial crisis of 2007–2008 that stripped many of their homes, there are more vacant houses than homeless citizens, will make you resist, even rebel against, the claim that everything is dandy. Perhaps, especially in this case if you're white, you'll vote for the only guy who admits that your leg has been peed on.

If you have the sense that this is an especially chaotic time in history, Marx would certainly agree. This is a time in which many people can see that they're being peed on, or, to go back to that more tasteful way of describing a historical shift, they can see their chains made visible.

You might have heard or read some version of this:

> The history of all hitherto existing society is the history of class struggles.
>
> Freeman and slave, patrician and plebeian, lord and serf, guild-master and journeyman, in a word, oppressor and oppressed, stood in constant opposition to one another, carried on an uninterrupted, now hidden, now open fight, a fight that each time ended, either in a revolutionary reconstitution of society at large, or in the common ruin of the contending classes.

These words, from *The Communist Manifesto*, which Marx wrote with his friend and lifelong patron Friedrich Engels, might seem dusty to you. We don't go about saying "guild-master" a lot these days. But, however old the description, history continues its habit of shifting the world from one form of organization to the next.

Since the Neolithic Age in the West, small-scale societies became larger ones. In Western prehistory, we lived in subsistence economies, where we made what we needed to survive. These became, in many cases, slave economies, where we made what a few others craved. When it became unfeasible to hold a growing population in chains, slave economies became feudal economies. The European serf was, if you like, the property of her lord. But she sometimes got a few days off to work the land of the lord's estate for her own use and to tend to her own needs and desires.

The land was worked by her and others so efficiently that productivity and the population grew. The growing serf population saw that they were in chains, which were imposed more fully by lords once they sensed their riches were in trouble. History made another organizational change and, after a few centuries and a few monarchs' heads, became capitalist.

We call capitalism a "mode of production," just as we would call a subsistence economy or a feudal economy or a slave economy the same. If you're a Marxist, you see the new slaves are workers. You see the new slave-masters are those on the *Forbes* rich list. You see the new slave-drivers as both the people that keep telling us that things are *great*, per Mrs. Obama, and those who tell us that we should just blame other slaves, per the racist Mr. Trump.

The mode of production evolves over time. What has tended to happen is that it has changed when its chains became visible and were broken during "class struggles," which occur when the majority class gets crapped off. Then the ruling class experiments with the nature of the chains and we move from one mode of production to the next. During these times, some crazy shit goes down.

We are in such a period right now. You are not, in my Marxist view, paranoid if you think things are currently weird. As the Marxist Antonio Gramsci put it in writing about Italian fascism in the 1930s, "the crisis consists precisely in the fact that the old is dying and the new cannot be born." In this time, he says, "a great variety of morbid symptoms appear." Trump is a morbid symptom.

You can say that all previous modes of production have given the world wonderful things. Small-scale subsistence economies gave people the opportunity to spend most of their time making complex culture, which, I imagine, is a very nice way to spend one's time. The slave mode gave us large structures that well-paid capitalist workers now go on vacations to see. It gave guys like Plato the opportunity to write elegant justifications for slavery. The feudal mode gave us castles, a growing population, and the inspiration for the soft incest porn seen on *Game of Thrones*.

Capitalism has given us *so much*. I won't even start listing its achievements, as (a) this would take all day, and (b) capitalism already has such a big head. Marx himself praised capitalism as a dynamic and productive force. He would have *loved the shit* out of factory robots. For Marx, capitalism is a necessary and painful stage in human development. And for Marx, it's about fucking time that we get on with the next stage — one that will guarantee our freedom, for all time, from chains.

Whatever Marx or Helen says about the need for a communist mode of production (not to be viewed as identical to the communist *states* we have seen; these *never* adopted a communist mode of production), the capitalist mode of production is dying. Trump is the morbid symptom of this long death.

I will tell you in the next chapter how, per Marx, capitalism is doomed to die. For the minute, trust me that the poor old mode of production is on its last legs, which is why it is peeing on everybody else's, by telling us all this is "great" or by blaming certain of its slaves. The biggest demographic swing to Trump came from poor people. More than fifty percent of US workers now earn less than thirty grand a year, which is *just* about enough dosh to eat and feel constantly shitty. It's true that more people in this big group voted for Clinton than for Trump, but fewer in this group voted for her than they had for any previous Democratic nominee. Clinton lost sixteen points of the party's traditional working poor votes; quite the achievement, especially when you consider that not all of these people were white: Trump, curious news, also received a boost from Hispanic voters. This guy. You know, the one that claimed that Mexico had a large population of enthusiastic rapists.

If Clinton had said convincingly, "I understand that you guys, whatever your color, are doing it tough, and I'm going to give you jobs repairing our terrible bridges," three things would have happened. One, Donald Trump would not have been elected president by citizens of the miserable flyover states. Two, people in those states would have jobs. Three, those shitty bridges across the United States would no longer be the stuff of an engineer's nightmare.

All she needed to increase her numbers was say that things were financially shitty for most of the people. She would not. Most of her party would not. Chuck Schumer, still a big player in the Democratic Party, out and out said that he didn't think chasing the poor vote was worthwhile. When asked by the press in 2016 if he was worried about polls that saw Clinton's numbers decline in poor counties, he said, "For every blue-collar Democrat we lose in western Pennsylvania, we will pick up two moderate Republicans in the suburbs in Philadelphia, and you can repeat that in Ohio and Illinois and Wisconsin."

As we all now know, that didn't work. You hardly need to be a Marxist to know that it couldn't, you just need to do some brutally simple logic: if a majority eligible to vote are having a shitty time, they are not going to be inclined to support the candidate who promises, "I refuse to acknowledge that you are having a shitty time." It is fucking amazing to me that Schumer said to the *Washington Post* that when "incomes decline, people tend to move in a more progressive direction."

When incomes decline, people move in *whatever* direction promises to move those incomes up. Trump was the only one of two nominees promising to do this. Loads of people voted for him. You don't need Marx to explain why people don't always become "progressive" when incomes fall. Chuck Schumer must be the only living American who has never seen a documentary on Hitler.

We must acknowledge that it wasn't just the impoverished workers of America who voted for Trump. There were plenty of white people of means that saw promise in his garbage. But even these people had experienced a decline in real wages, and you may now personally know how financial anxiety can cause people to do dumb and desperate stuff. In my adult life, I have been sufficiently underemployed and broke to cause me to lash out at others. I have, in low times, imagined that others were "stealing" my work.

This is dumb, of course. The Marxist must remember our labor is always stolen by the capitalist race to profit, and *never* by other workers. Still, even in my Marxist head, I did dumb stuff. Many US workers did dumb stuff, too, and this was expressed as racism, a convenient old form of bigotry.

None of this racism was reasonable, of course. Racism is nothing if not the most total defiance of reason. To see the undocumented Mexican laborer as the source of your trouble is unreasonable. After all, she works in a job with conditions so bad you'd never agree to them. To see the Chinese laborer as the source of your trouble is unreasonable. After all, the low prices of the goods you can afford to buy at Walmart are only made possible by her slavery. To believe that black or brown people are going to invade your home is unreasonable. After all, in the United States of today, the person most likely to invade your home and steal your shit is a debt collector.

All these are delusions. They make no sense if you think them through. But all these delusions are easier than facing the difficult, more complicated truth, which was not being addressed at all by Clinton's Democrats. America is great, remember, and don't let anyone ever tell you otherwise. This is a lie that many people can easily perceive as a lie with their senses. The truth can only be honestly addressed by someone who is at least moderately influenced by Marx.

Marx was the first guy to really write down an account of how poverty and insecurity are the inevitable results of capitalism, a system he says has internal contradictions — again, more on this super fun topic in the next chapter. But to sum up my pinko raving for now: if no one dares to publicly blame capitalism for poverty, as was the case in the 2016 US election, someone else will be held by the masses to account: blacks, Muslims, Mexicans, women, Chinese factory workers.

Donald Trump addressed wealth inequality, which is real and widespread in the United States, a number of times. Between all the vile sexism, racism, and mockery, he did pause to address what his Democratic opponent would not: the vastly diminished "greatness" of the American experience. At one point, he even addressed an economic question to black American voters on Twitter: "What the hell do you have to lose?"

The answer, in a cultural sense, is of course, "All respect for my people within the public conversation." But this wasn't a cultural question. It was a question of material wealth to which the true answer, sadly, is, "Most of us are already poor, and Hillary is not promising to address this. So, in wallet terms, we stand to lose nothing." There were black voters utterly repulsed by Trump's racism, but also so utterly beset by poverty that they were prepared to roll the dice.

Can you *really* say to all the Trump voters, even those of color, that this gamble was made from stupidity or malice alone?

Have you *never* looked to a false and easy solution in a time of fear? Have you never been so poor that you decided to make a desperate bet?

Trump is, save for Bernie Sanders, the only US presidential candidate in many decades to publicly utter the term "working class." Despite his use of a classically Marxist term, Donald Trump is in no way a Marxist. He has been called a fascist, and while I'm not convinced this is an accurate or a helpful description of his crazed neo-nationalism, let's just call him one, not only because it feels good, but because it permits me to offer up a good quote, which is, "Every rise of fascism bears witness to a failed revolution."

This translated remark is attributed to Walter Benjamin, a German Marxist forced to flee his own nation's fascism while Hitler was on the campaign trail. The guy knew fascism firsthand. He saw two possible popular responses to a time of great economic recession, such as the people of Germany faced in 1933 and we face right now. This is what he means: you can build a revolution that seeks to address the economic problem at the root of the economic crisis, *or* you can wait for some shouty simpleton who loudly blames it all on the Jews/Muslims/Mexicans/homosexuals/communists/uppity women.

What will *not* work to persuade anyone much at all in a time of economic crisis is a claim like, "Don't let anyone ever tell you that this depressed and broken Weimar Republic isn't great!"

I hotly agree with Benjamin that these become the only two possibilities in times of inevitable capitalist crisis. The choice we now face, to use the old communist slogan made popular by a gal called Rosa Luxemburg, is "socialism or barbarism." Fascism or revolution.

In the Marxist view, it doesn't matter how badly you regard Trump voters. You *can* think badly of them, sure. I have dreadful thoughts about them myself. Whenever I am forced into conversation with a person of the type, my instinct is to punch them. It is my personal view that it is probably enormous fun to punch a fascist or a fascist sympathizer. But, it is my Marxist view that a mass punching of people who vote for fascists is itself an act largely of self-gratification. I am not saying individual violence is always bad; sometimes, in your personal life, it may be the only recourse. State violence, on the other hand, is *never* pardonable. The violence of the state, and its partner capitalist economy, is the true violence a Marxist seeks to combat. Not an end achieved, as you may come to agree, by punching one or two loudmouth fascists from 4chan.

So, you can think dreadful things about the people who vote for Trump. You can call them, as Hillary Clinton did, "deplorable." You can, if you're a nice, compassionate type, "reach out" to them and try to explain to them the error of their ways. (Don't try this. They'll call you a politically correct elite and refuse to listen, and possibly say mean things about you at one of their tedious lectures.) Or, you could consider that the choices we face are as they have long been in the economically depressed liberal democratic state: fascism or revolution; socialism or barbarism.

You may continue to despair and write hashtags and call out racism and Trumpism online. Punch a Nazi. Wear a safety pin. But, do so knowing that changing the *ideas* of people is never going to be as effective as changing, or attempting to change, the *material* conditions of people. Again, Clinton made *no consistent promise* that she would do this. *Again*, I am not saying that Clinton is the devil or "even worse than Trump." I am simply stating, in Marxist terms, what history tends to produce: reactions.

And now it's time to hit you with a Classic Marxist Memory. It's a tune with a very clumsy name, but I need you to sing it so

we can stop the fascist barbarians. It's called "historical materialism." Historical materialism addresses the question of why things
change. It can answer our cries of "what the actual fuck?" When
the Marxist considers any historical shift in ideas — and we're currently undergoing a big one — she looks at the material conditions.

By material conditions, we first mean the stuff that keeps
you alive, then the stuff that keeps you happy or content. Like a
Maslow's hierarchy of needs–type deal. First, there's your shelter,
your food, your access to water — all actual problems for many
people in America who have faced foreclosure, a nutrition crisis,
and poisoned waterways. (Here in Australia, questions like housing affordability, underemployment and increased cost of education are currently among our most urgent. These are certainly
creating an emerging consciousness in the group impacted by
them the most: Millennials.) Next, there are those less pressing
needs, such as your production of culture, objects, and meaningful
bonds with others. Life, as that Walter guy wrote, is "a fight for the
crude and material things without which no refined and spiritual
things could exist."

The Marxist looks at the terrain of these material conditions,
then sees how certain ideas can grow there, and how these ideas
can, in turn, lead to new material conditions.

If nearly all speech and writing everywhere is any guide, this is
the *opposite* of how most people in the West currently think. Many
believe that the *idea* exists *first*, and *then* produces a *material result*.
They will say, for example, "Racism causes poverty," or, "Workplace
bullying exists only because many people have bad ideas."

This mode of thought was born from a long Western lineage.
Stay with me here as I give you a brief look at this tradition. I know
philosophy can be very boring, but I'll try to make it quick.

To think that the idea starts everything is the way many people have thought of the world for millennia. They say that the perception, or the *idea* of a thing, comes before *material* reality. It's like the old, "If a tree falls in the forest and no one hears it, did it really fall?" thing.

If you think that material reality can be said to exist *only* as the result of perception, you are, technically, an "idealist." If you think, "Fuck, of course the tree made a sound. Do you expect me to be everywhere monitoring all environmental crimes at all times?" you are a "materialist." When we use the word *idealist* here it's not in the everyday sense, to mean someone with their head in the clouds. And, when we use the word *materialist* here, we do not mean it in the everyday sense, to mean someone with their head in the Nordstrom catalogue.

Now, even though you might be a rational person who is happy to let climate scientists report on the falling of trees without recording their sound, you may still be, in some respects, an idealist if, for example, you say workplace bullying is just the result of bad ideas — we say "people have bad ideas" and do not consider that bad conditions produced these bad ideas. A Marxist, who is a materialist, will say that workplace bullying exists because *what the shit else would you expect* when labor conditions are so unequal. The conditions of the workplace produce the bullying. Bullying is part of any workplace under capitalism, and we shouldn't be surprised by it. It's not just bad people with bad ideas that result in your workplace torture.

This does not mean the bullying is excused by a Marxist. It just means it is largely *understood* in terms of its material history. The Marxist, AKA a *historical* materialist, does not deny the role of the idea in the terrible workplace action. She just sees it as part of a historical interaction with the material.

Marx believes that ideas come from somewhere in material history, that they do not simply arise on their own. After all, starving people can't think straight, or for very long at all before they kick it. As he writes in *The Grundrisse*, ideas are "directly *interwoven* with the material activity and the material intercourse of men, the language of real life" (my emphasis). History's conversation between the worker and her workplace conditions produces the bullying behavior. History's conversation between the material and the idea is what can produce a fascist like Trump, and the racism that supports him.

History for the Marxist is thought of as an elaborate carpet being made. We don't claim to be able to predict the placement of all its threads. What we *do* get as Marxists is a bit of a knitting pattern. Many of us did say "socialism or barbarism" in the countdown to the US election, and warned that Trump would be elected. We said, "This has happened before." We repeated Marx's old zinger from 1852: history's facts and persons tend to appear twice, "the first time as tragedy, the second time as farce."

What I am going to describe to you now is a very important part of Marx's thinking. It's also, perhaps, the second- or third-most mind-fucking part. I did wonder whether it was a bit mean of me to bring this complicated thing up for you so soon, but I truly think this is the first step in understanding Marx: the idea and the material are actually *interwoven*.

I should own up and tell you that a lot of Marxists disagree that this is the place to start, or even a thing to consider at all. They dismiss historical materialism as bullshit. These folks just say material conditions are the starting point for everything else, including art, customs and concepts of gender and ethnicity. I once even heard a Marxist on the *Q&A* TV show say "Culture doesn't really exist."

This is extreme materialism. It is not historical materialism. In my view, such a Marxist skips not only over observable fact — of course culture fucking exists — but every part of Marx where the production of "spiritual and refined things" get a big thumbs-up, and the parts where Marx himself explicitly states the interplay between the material and the idea.

Historical materialism describes this interplay. In 1857, Marx first calls the material way in which we organize our societies the "base" and the way in which these base conditions are managed — chiefly, law and politics, but it can be other stuff as well — the "superstructure." I'm sure you've worked it out by now, but let me make it plain: the base corresponds to the *material* and the super-structure to the *ideal*.

There are those Marxists who are very rigid with their under-standing of this relation — it will probably not surprise you to learn that it was this kind of "scientific socialism" that informed some of the most brutal Soviet leaders. This understanding that everything comes *only* from the base continues to dazzle some Marxists of the present, like the *Q&A* guy, and you might have recently seen some of these people say, "Poor white people in America are racist only because of their poverty."

People who are the object of racism get very shitty when they hear this rationale, and so they should. This form of Marxism holds that people have no agency, that you can't blame the poor widdle racists. All very well and good until you yourself are subject to bigotry.

I mean, *yes*, the base is very influential, and its hard ground can propagate an awful weed like racism. But, I don't think Marx con-cludes that It's All About That Base. Because, if he did, we all may as well give up, right? If everything we do, including yelling racist shit, is determined by material history, why bother changing? We're all robots led only by the movement of history, so let's give up on the idea of resistance. We'll resist when history tells us to.

This view, which might be called "deterministic" by philosophers, is pretty depressing. It was not Marx's view. (*Okay.* He did write some polemics in his youth that could be read this way. But he was a kid just trying shit out. I once dyed my hair magenta in my twenties. We can all make bold and unflattering style statements when young.)

The traffic between the base and the superstructure, the material and the idea, goes both ways. Marx *says* this, and I think we can see this when we look at the racism that has grown over time in America and which became so influential in the 2016 election.

Historical materialism *could* be a challenge to the way you currently think about things, including the racist horror of the present. You might think that we build the material world based only on a bad idea. You might think the reason that black people in America experience such disproportionate poverty is due to racist ideas. This is true, but it's only a portion of the two-way story. If we look at the history of racist ideas in the United States of America, we see that they have their origins in the material United States.

Let's have a bit of a look through the Marxist spyglass at how the material and the idea, the base and the superstructure, interweave in this case. You do not have to like or sympathize with racists, okay? But, you may find, when you consider the historical materialist account of racism and its political and economic uses in the United States, that you need a better explanation for the 2016 election result than, "People just need to have better ideas"; i.e., the Clinton and Obama view. We need more than better ideas. We need people to live in better material conditions, right?

We're talking history here, comrades, so this could have been a *super* long story of US racism, instead of just the *quite* long one I offer here. We *could* go back in time to the colonial racism of old Europe, imported to America by Columbus and first tragically expressed on what would become US soil as a massacre of the Timucua peoples in 1539. I don't want, at all, to overlook the brutal seizure of First Nations' life and land, or the cruel history of the colonizers. But, we've got to choose a place to start this conversation. With respect to our First Nations comrades, let this starting point be the Declaration of Independence.

To build wealth in a nation-state he claimed to have founded on "Life, Liberty and the pursuit of Happiness," Thomas Jefferson needed to validate denying all these things to the two hundred black people he owned, and the countless people whose lives were claimed and abased by his peers.

The terrible idea of black inferiority, as invented by the wealthy, took hold as fast as chains. When black men became free men in 1865 (I'm not being sexist; women were, in fact, left out of the story) the majority poor whites, having heard racist ideas expressed by slave masters all their lives, saw a threat to their material existence. Black workers, of course, *could* have been a real "threat" to white workers in the nineteenth century. They *could* have been competing for the same jobs, had they been truly freed within the limited terms that capitalism's "free" market allows.

But instead there was the legal and the cultural maintenance of racism, a superstructure created by wealthy slave owners eager to preserve both their profits and their view of themselves as noble: following abolition, most black people continued to work in jobs that were almost identical to slavery, thanks to the racist *idea*. It wasn't for another century that black Americans were able to meaningfully protest the remnants of law, the superstructure, that kept them in twentieth-century chains. A large part of the reason they *could* protest this shit was America's new prosperity (a *material* thing, just in case you'd lost your way), of which quasi-Marxist policies, called the New Deal, had allowed them to share in just a little.

Martin Luther King Jr. was murdered in 1968 while addressing a group of black sanitation workers, who had assembled to protest their material conditions. These people would never have gathered together if the material conditions of the time had not produced mass employment, labor that had been racially divided because of those old racist ideas. Put a whole lot of seriously fucked-over black people in one workplace and give them a *little* money and what happens? They will create a new idea. A good one, which in this case was: Pony up, you hypocrites. If this really is a country where "all men are created equal," let's get to it. Equal pay. Equal labor rights. *Real* suffrage. And while you're at it, stop using those foul words, created by centuries of material and idea interweaving, that remind me that you think equality is not my entitlement. Don't reduce me with your *ideas*. Don't diminish me with shit *material* conditions.

If you read Martin Luther King Jr., you will find that he had a historical materialist bent. White liberals prefer to remember him as a man who just spoke about "dreams," our nocturnal ideas, but if you look up that famous speech you'll find it contains reference to the material poverty of people in its first seconds.

The powerful speech of people like MLK moved many black people to action, and effectively challenged the prejudices of some white people, as well. It was not just the ideas MLK communicated that prompted some white people — including Bernie

Sanders — to join Civil Rights action. It was the material conditions of the time, as well. Then, the white middle class in the US
was growing. Unemployment was low and living conditions had
never been higher for whites. So, a comfortable white person who
gave the matter of black people's legal and cultural oppression
some thought in this time was likely to be more generous and reasonable. You have a job, enough to eat, and kids with a future full
of hope and you have seen how nice it is to live in a community
with people who also have these things; you are more inclined to
want it for everyone.

Their survival, after all, had never been truly threatened by
blacks. Others clung to the idea that black people were lazy. From
about the time of the American Civil War to the last quarter of the
twentieth century, most white American workers had lived lives
that were markedly better than those of their parents. White people
learned to suppose that the natural material direction was up, and
that any person who didn't follow that path was lazy. They justified
systematic cruelty in the same way Jefferson had.

But some of them became a little more opposed to racism. This
was due not just to their material comfort, but to the powerful ideas
of people like MLK, Huey P. Newton, and Malcolm X. Many white
people marched with their black comrades, sickened by the history
of racism and emboldened to protest. These allies were the white
Boomers, a historically fortunate middle class who had Maslow's list
checked off and then some. We give the Boomers shit, but we'd do
well to remember that many of them took hold of history with the
power of solidarity and changed it for the better in the 1960s.

By the time the 1980s rolled 'round, wages for most people had
begun to stagnate. Still, America, particularly *white* America, re-
tained a clear vision of itself as a place of opportunity. Even though

jobs became scarce and poorly paid, the idea, formed over a century, that you would always do better than your parents, remained strong. If you failed, you were lazy.

Gradually, welfare was stripped from all people — the K.O. was delivered in 1996 by Bill Clinton, with the *Personal Responsibility and Work Opportunity Act*. Global trade and technical innovation did away with the jobs. Black and Hispanic Americans had always had it bad, so this was nothing new for them. At least, no huge descent. But by 2016, white people were in a state of shock, with their wages having dropped, by proportion, the most.

During this period of decline, which has now reached a critical point, US administrations promised a better material tomorrow. When the better tomorrow failed to arrive, US administrations announced that it was here in any case. "The economy is growing!" "Productivity is up!" The wage decline, most acute for formerly comfortable whites, was said not to exist.

The white underclass was beginning to get the idea, thanks to material conditions, that they were thought of as lazy. They felt the bigotry. The way that they may have thought of black people — as unwilling to make it in this "great" nation and so responsible for their own misfortune — was now the way they were construed by leaders who kept insisting that this country was *full* of opportunity. This was made very clear even in the title of Clinton's Act: it's your "personal responsibility" to fix the fact of mass unemployment. Fucking "personal responsibility." Marxists get very cranky when they hear this term, because they know it's a lie: policymakers create certain conditions that coerce us into living in a certain way, then tell us it's our "responsibility" to overcome them.

The white working class now feel the frustration long accepted as a fact of life by the black working class. Leaders keep saying,

"You can make it if you try!" Yet your experience tells you something very different. In the space between the material (failing to make ends meet) and the idea (politicians telling you that you can make it if you dream big), you conclude you are being called a loser. You are, in other words, being treated at a systemic level in the same way you may have personally thought of black people. You kept thinking that they could make it only if they tried. Now, you're trying and you can't make it.

In an economic sense, and in a psychological one, too, the majority of the white population in the United States felt an unfamiliar pain and a great confusion. They had lost so much. They were told, as black people had been since the end of slavery, that *they* were responsible for their own difficult lives.

During slavery, black people heard no justification whatsoever. They were simply held in chains. When the chains came off, they were called "lazy" or criminal or whatever the superstructure needed to say to reassert its relationship with the capitalist base. We heard some slightly updated versions of this during the Trump campaign. Black and brown people were, again, called criminal. Black and brown activists were described as intellectually lazy, always with the "politically correct" language and never wanting to do an honest day's work and so on and so on.

The noble idea for a white working-class person to have had in 2016 would have been, "My black comrades and I are as one and will fight this inequality together." Instead, racial divisions were revived and exploited by Donald Trump, and material divisions denied by Michelle Obama, who offered the idea that America was already "great."

The candidate Bernie Sanders, who had stood with his black comrades in the 1960s, did begin to utter the noble idea. He agreed with Mrs. Obama that racism was a terrible force and also agreed with Mr. Trump that wage inequality was a terrible force. Having some familiarity with Marx's thinking, Sanders could see things as black and white at once; as *both* idea and material reality. But a lot of folks who prefer a *just* black or *just* white way of thinking supposed that Sanders, in implicitly disagreeing with Mrs. Obama that America was "great," had sympathy for racists. In understanding the pain of those who had lost the most, as well as the pain of those who had always had the least, he was seen by some as an apologist for awful white guys.

The Marxist doesn't have to apologize for, or even like, a particular group of people to understand that "freedom for each" is also "freedom for all." Freedom, to exist at all, must be afforded to *everyone*, even awful white guys on minimum wages who voted for Trump.

This Marxist plea is not to understand or empathize with the individual racist, the bigot, the homophobe, but rather it is to understand the conditions in which a bad idea like racism thrives. It is to be committed to freedom for all. Yes. This includes fuckwits.

Hillary Clinton's campaign strategists *must* have known that most Americans had experienced real wage decline for forty years. They must have known that the greatest decline in income had occurred among white men, who still earned more than their black and Hispanic fellows, but had lost more nonetheless. They must have known that a previous agreement, such as President Clinton's North American Free Trade Agreement (NAFTA) — which facilitated the movement of jobs to other nations — an agreement so hated, people actually bothered to remember its name. To be fair, it was actually that old tool Ronald Reagan who got this insecure labor thing rolling — an era of policy we now call "neoliberal." But Bill gave it an enthusiastic shove with the superstructure.

Clinton herself *knew* that young people in particular were hurting, often unable to secure a home or a sustainable job. In a leaked recording of a 2015 fundraiser, she can be heard to describe the "children of the Great Recession" as "living in their parents' basement," working as "baristas" and without "much of a future."

Ugh. I find this speech abhorrent. First, how dare anyone malign baristas? Baristas, especially those who relish their work, are like gods to me and deserve *all* the luxury and freedom in the world for their fine pour. Without good coffee, people get incredibly angry, as they did during the East German Coffee Crisis of the late 1970s. That shortage nearly brought down the state; and, no, I'm not kidding.

More importantly, Clinton accidentally described the 2007–2008 crash as it was, and what a Marxist would call it: the beginning of a great recession. *But she didn't see this as a significant problem.* She conceded that many people had been trapped by it. She just didn't think addressing it was that important, or the way to win the election. Perhaps she thought all these basement dwellers were too depressed to vote. She certainly thought she could win by promising only to be *not* Donald Trump. A fair bet, granted.

In the meantime, that tangerine fuck-ball was visiting rust-belt states and addressing crowds whose size quickly began to outstrip Clinton's — although they were never half the size of Bernie's. He went to places with names Clinton didn't know and, while she enlisted the aid of glamorous and compassionate celebrities, he set about directly courting those basement-dwelling voters the Democrats had decided to forget. He didn't win the popular vote. He won, as was his aim, the electoral college. He won the historical lottery.

Marx, the historical materialist, tells us that particular economic conditions can create a particular political response. He is fucking right. In a Marxist reading of history, Trump makes sense. Whereas in the idealist reading — remember, that's when you think ideas are the single driving force of history — Trump makes no sense, a Marxist finds his appearance disgusting but logical. An idealist finds it aberrant. Idealists keep saying, "I don't understand how these ideas happened." Historical materialists say, "I told you so."

I've been holding on to it for a while, but now I'll give you the big quote from old Karl-o:

> It is not the consciousness of men that determines their being, but, on the contrary, their social being that determines their consciousness.

Read that again. I'll wait. It's awesome.

Walter Benjamin, the man who thought in both black and white, knew this, too. He was there for the rise of Hitler and despaired for the absence of a materially focused politics, AKA Marxism, that could have done away with that foul fascist splotch, and all his execrable, murdering playdates. During great recessions — and the greatest of these directly preceded the Nazis' rise — fascism steps in when socialism hasn't got its trousers on yet.

Blame the Jews. Blame the Muslims. Blame those hoity-toity gays. So long as you are, during a time of great economic hardship such as we currently face, blaming *someone*, you're in with a good chance at power. Just don't charge *all* people with the responsibility for the shit they find themselves in. If you say, as Mrs. Obama did, that there's no one to blame because nothing is wrong, you tend, in times of downturn, to get downturned.

This was the Democratic Party's mistake: to believe that they could sell barely defined ideas about America and greatness to people who face great personal debt and uncertainty. Mrs. Obama believed, as did her fellows, that talking about some sort of vague camaraderie was enough to bind people together. The Marxist believes that people on their own tend to place more value on a decent life than on "values," and that people can only truly be bound together under capitalism in the fight for that decent life. Our lives shape our attachment to certain values. This is what the Marxist believes; and, it is knowledge that the fascist, always ready to steal our revolution, has learned to exploit. "It's all just great! Don't ever let anyone tell you that it's not!" Mrs. Obama, you will doubtless long remain your nation's most gracious First Lady, but, as a glance at any US wealth inequality graph will tell you, that is such a bunch of shit. It's a bunch of shit that Trump exploited. The idealists of the Democratic Party made a grave error in allowing Trump to tell so many lies about the United States through their unwillingness to confront the economic truth. To quote Julia Roberts from the not-particularly-Marxist film *Pretty Woman*: "Big mistake. Huge."

You can justifiably charge us Marxists with many big mistakes. Huge. We've made the women get the morning tea while the men of the vanguard talked about posh stuff. We've been racist, or pretended that race meant nothing. We've not respected our comrades' gender, sexuality, or faith. There was also, of course, that whole thing with Stalin, who always, to my irritation, claimed to be a Marxist, instead of a guy who gave the people state capitalism and lied, "Presto, perfect communism!" But one thing we've rarely done is believe that things are just "great!"

We don't think things are great, or that, under capitalism, they can ever be great for long or for more than a handful of people in a handful of nations. This is why we use phrases like "the bosses" and "the workers" and can generally be heard complaining about those who cruelly extract profit from the bodies of the laborers. The harshness of most people's material lives is a pretty big deal for us, and we're *super* into the notion that these material conditions, whether they are lived or reasonably feared, produce our ideas, which, in turn, can create new material conditions.

If you're living in the shitter and all you have is fascism as the expression of your political consciousness, then the fascist idea is what you might choose. Ergo, we Marxists think you'd better help us get our Marxist shit together *right now*. Because here we are, in a time when very few people want to elect those nice centrist parties, like Clinton's Democrats, who just keep saying that things are "great" even when they privately admit that they're not.

These leaders know we are living in a basement. Hillary knew it. In her leaked 2015 fundraising speech, Hillary even goes on to say that she understands why basement-dwellers might want something different, and she chuckles as she mentions Bernie's "revolution." She just wasn't prepared to cede only a tiny part of that revolution's aims to the baristas. She thought she could put the idea — in her case, a vague idea about a loving and inclusive America full of those who took "personal responsibility" — before the material reality. A Marxist knows this to be a mistake.

Donald Trump was not, regrettably, too stupid to intuit one basic tenet of Marxism: changed material conditions force a change in political opinion. If you listen to some of Trump's campaign speeches, you'll see that he echoed, albeit quite feebly, the anti–big bank sentiments of Bernie Sanders. He knew that life in a basement could produce a particular political concern. He made a show of addressing it.

This is the thing about the modern fascist. They all seem to know that material conditions come first, and ideas after. And so they speak, very often, like Marxists. That is, when they're not using racism with the tongue otherwise busy cleaning the devil's asshole.

Donald Trump's administration is *very* unlikely to improve present material conditions for the many any more than Clinton's would have. Unemployment and underemployment will continue to rise. Guys from the c-suites of Wall Street and Silicon Valley will remain in charge, both within the White House and outside it. What we have in Trump is the worst of all possible political combinations: grossly intolerant speech that conceals a grossly unfair economic regime. With Clinton, we would have had tolerant speech that concealed a grossly unfair economic regime. The liberal — that is, an idealist who believes that liberal democracy is basically fine — thinks that the Clinton version is preferable. The Marxist looks at the problem and says, "Hmm. This situation is both black and white."

Of course, on an emotional level, it is very easy to make the case for the pleasant centrism of Hillary Clinton. Even if we know that she is intimately involved with Goldman Sachs and other companies who were both the beneficiaries and the cause of the great recession that dropped many of us down to the basement. Because at least she has the decency to *seem* like a nice person — other than when she is calling people deplorable, basement-dwelling baristas, in semiprivate speeches.

Clinton is nicer. I'm not being entirely sarcastic, here. The speed and breadth with which Trump has taken a shit on public conversation sickens me. If we must have US neoliberalism that afflicts all nations, and brutal flying-robot foreign policy to boot, we might as well have it served up with an American smile.

But the Marxist grits her teeth, ground down while fretting about how un-great everything is, and remembers that she's spent years preparing for this naked moment. People are now rejecting traditional capitalism — opting in some cases for the fascist and in others for the socialist. It's not a choice for us anymore between the nice centrist and the ugly racist. Both are unacceptable. Both views will continue to inform each other throughout history unless the Marxist intervenes — liberalism and fascism are not the enemies they think they are, but historically material partners. Capitalism, even the liberal kind, will eventually produce a fascist. When the fascist begins to emerge, we know that it's time for socialism. Which must not fail to free the people again.

Freedom. What a baffling turd of a word. Revolution. What a difficult concept. Historical materialism, ugh. "Helen, why are you making me learn stupid new phrases?" Because if you don't want the barbaric fascists our material history has produced, you'd better get learning.

What you may have learned to this point is that it is your "personal responsibility" to change your life, and even those of others, for the better. What the Marxist learns is that the people, each and all, must join to take hold of history in the moment. Anything else is a farce.

**2**

---

## So, Like, Marx Totally Told You This Would Happen! And HE Didn't Even Have A "Flip Cell Phone"!

---

am a very clumsy person. And *no*, don't worry, I'm not going to argue that my clumsiness can be somehow explained by capitalism. To be clear, we commies don't blame capitalism for *everything*. Only the violent seizure of our creative instincts, about ninety percent of the bigotry in the world, and of our very selves by the ruling class. I mean, sure, capitalism has led to the owner-ship, death, and demonization of billions, but we cannot say that it caused Helen to become a klutz. This is just a flaw in my genetic software — or a "feature," as the companies of Silicon Valley so often rebrand their mistakes.

So. As a very clumsy person, I recently tried to delay my inev-itable murder of a new smartphone by buying a bouncy cover for it. This piece of fucking plastic, the only one guaranteed to fit my Pixel (yes, I *know* — I gave my money and all my potentially profit-able data to Google, capitalism's most successful monster) cost me sixty dollars. Sixty dollars! That's about three hours of my labor. I chose not to open the invoice and remind myself of the total cost, but I recall that the shipping fee was quite high, too.

Apparently, this piece of bouncy plastic had to be dispatched to my crib in Australia from Singapore, where it wasn't even made. I don't know in which nation or under which conditions it *was* made, but I am confident that the answers are, respectively, "Somewhere in the Global South," and, "Pretty shitty." (But, the an-swer could very soon be "By a robot in a sexy sky factory," or "On my 3D printer." We'll get to the changes automation will bring. But here's the Marxist spoiler: the era of sexy robots will lead to the end of capitalism.)

We've all likely had an equivalent of this bouncy plastic experi-ence, the feeling of being ripped off at some point. We've thought, "That's ridonculous," when we've paid too much for some gadget or service or part. Sometimes capitalism shows itself to be very inefficient, and not just in its overpriced Google phone cases. In sectors like health, education, incarceration, and climate science, private capitalists spend a *load* more cash and produce far stingi-er results than the state capitalist institutions that once dared to manage, such matters. Private capitalism, even in its own terms, provides very poor value. Think of the unearthly environmental expenses it spews, then the cash it requests to mitigate them. Think of the Global Financial Crisis, where the US government's cash redress was put straight into the hands of the very financial institutions that caused it. What even *was* that bailout?

As you've asked, I'll tell you what it was: a reward to an emperor toddler for knowingly taking a dump on our kingdom's best rug. "Oh, you've soiled the Persian carpet? Here, little man, have the Bayeux Tapestry and go to the toilet on that next time. Now let me wipe your dainty bot-bot with this bundle of newly minted bonds."

Few establishment politicians care to admit that the leaders of the finance sector are privileged babies informed by a flimsy myth. Remember, Obama and Clinton were in complete support of the bailout. Rather than face the critical failures of late capitalism, politicians use taxpayer money to prop it up. If they gave the works of Marx, the great theorist of crisis, just half an afternoon's attention, they'd see that a capitalist economy can never achieve equilibrium, but is always destined to generate crises before eventually eating its own tail.

This is what we're going to blabber on about in this chapter: the crisis tendencies of capitalism itself. We're not going to talk so much about how capitalism is rotten from a moral standpoint here; we're going to diagnose its economic failings. Marxists are, of course, most absolutely cranky with the way capitalism disposes of and disregards so many human lives. But, Marxists are also fairly certain that capitalism has contradictions that will lead to its failure.

Despite clear evidence that our "too big to fail" institutions are simply too big and too reckless to exist at all, many folks maintain a view that private capitalism is a lean and efficient system. It *is* true that this system of organization produces and delivers us a lot of things with great efficiency, and often at a low, low price. If we exclude things like education, housing, health care, military equipment, climate science, sustainable food production, and other expensive trifles that only a politically correct snowflake like me would whimper about, private capitalism really does otherwise give us some super cheap shit. The T-shirt I wear today, for example, cost three dollars. Again, I don't *want* to trace the history of this T-shirt, which was brought to my home at no charge via an offshore clothing warehouse. But I know enough. I know that the worker who affixed the "Made in Bangladesh" label to its seam was exploited. She might have even been one of those many who died in the big Rana Plaza factory building collapse — yep, our T-shirts could be the work of a comrade who is now deceased. I know that the worker who packed it in Britain was exploited, maybe even strip-searched on the way out the door of the warehouse. That the Australian worker who brought it to my door was exploited. That the worker who now wears it is exploited — if I were not exploited, I would be able to afford something that I could at least be certain was made with union labor. I don't want to buy a T-shirt whose manufacture hurt someone. Dammit, I don't want such T-shirts to be made in such conditions at all. This T-shirt is a textile with a worker at both ends. Between these threads, just a few ruling-class folks are unravelling a marvelous profit.

You will be unsurprised to learn that a Marxist thinks that someone is always getting ripped off under capitalism. What *may* surprise you is that Marx wrote often with admiration about the way in which capitalism could produce and distribute so much — for a while. Even in *The Communist Manifesto*, Marx's most populist work and one in which capitalism comes across like a covetous devil with bloody fangs of gold, you get the feeling he is thinking, "The speed of this beast is pretty impressive!" I mean, it *really* is, in many ways. Sure, private capitalism has been historically awful at building roads at a reasonable cost, but it's been pretty good at inventing those things that drive on them. The true Marxist does *not* say that private capitalism has brought us nothing of worth. The true Marxist does not say that state capitalism has brought us nothing of worth; that would be a lie, as any economist who measures the unprecedented early economic growth of the USSR — which, again, was not communist but controlled state capitalism — would be forced to agree. We say, thanks for the rate of technological and social progress, thanks for those many things with the potential to improve all our lives. But we also say, especially when that speed starts hurting us in large numbers, it's time for one of those "cost-benefit analyses" capitalism itself is so fond of. What's the point of abundance and tech if so few of us get to share it? Let's take our foot off the capitalist pedal before we collide with a future that has no way to sustain us.

One of capitalism's fastest marvels occurred after Marx's death. The beardy guy would have *pooped* himself as he observed the rise of the motorcar. If Marx had seen the way Henry Ford did business, he would have written several kilograms of very angry, very fascinated book about it. He would have said, "I'm telling you, the car thing is marvelous, but this whole way of doing things must end! Make sure it ends well! Seize the factory! Seize back your own labor!" (Marx was quite fond of exclamation points in his pamphlets.)

Many non-Marxist businesspeople have written admiringly of Henry Ford. They even name a business era in his honor: Fordism.

Some of these admirers, which include Donald Trump, even think we can go back to Fordism. Oh, lol.

Fordism refers to the way in which the labor in early twentieth-century Western factories was often organized. Ford wasn't the first to assign unskilled people different assembly jobs, thereby maximizing efficiency; but, he did it on what was then considered a monumental scale. His workers belched *millions* of cars.

The term also refers to the subsequent low cost of production, which enabled the workers, well paid by Ford, to buy those very same automobiles. Which, if you think about it, was *amazing*. Imagine the time of your great- or possibly great-great-great-grandparents: people frequently owned little more than two suits of clothes and the contents of their stomachs. In just a matter of years, many people working in these new conditions could afford the marvel of a *motorcar*. It makes the modern magic of Uber seem like a secondhand tricycle by contrast, right?

So, Ford was famous for paying his workers quite well. He is also infamous for being a racist shithead, who wrote some truly dreadful things about blacks and Jews in his correspondence. Man, he was one racist tool. But, this guy paid his black workers the same as his white workers at a time when very few other entrepreneurs thought to offer race wage equality.

It's interesting to pause here, wearing the fancy historical materialist hat we tried on in the last chapter — remember that stuff I was going on about, wherein an idea like racism could be formed and upheld in large part by material conditions? Well, in this case, material conditions hit the pause button on some elements of racism. It wasn't because Henry was good, but because racism would have been a bad business decision for him. Sometimes, racism is good for business. Sometimes, it's bad. The point for us Marxists is to *not* allow business this power of influence on ideas, however it is wielded. Like, it's all very well and good that Apple today wants marriage equality or whatever, but why in the name of sweet fuck are we permitting large companies to influence our moral decisions? If Coca-Cola can bring us tolerance, it can also bring us intolerance. The point is, companies whose internal "democracies" are devised by those who own the most should not have the power to make moral decisions.

Ford was a guy who accidentally enabled a great flourishing of African American culture and community in the city of Detroit. He was also a guy who loved to use the N-word. Ford suspended his racism when it came to business. Not because he was nice; he was, as we have already established, a total shithead. Rather, it was because he knew that if he paid his black workers enough, they could afford to buy his stuff, and that they would in turn encourage others in their communities to buy his stuff, as per the famous Fordist model. I am certain that if it had been plausible and efficient for Ford to charge black workers one price for a car and white workers another, he would have. It was not. My Marxist point here is, any virtue that comes from the Ford example, or any other business example, is not intentional. It is all in the service of maximizing quick manufacturing, distribution, sale, and profit.

This means a racist tool might organize the racism out of his factory, but *only if it is profitable to do so.* If racism works for profit, he'll organize it back in — by many accounts, Toyota, a company we'll look at next, exploited sexist and racist bigotry in its labor force to keep the production lines moving. Profit is the capitalist's true motivation. It has to be. Yes, it is even the motivation for apparently nice guys like Bill Gates, who we'll certainly have a bash at in a later chapter. *Please* remember this: the way our material lives as workers are organized — what we have to eat, where we get to sleep, how much pleasure we take from our labor — is the way our entire lives, and our ideas about them, become organized. It's the material stuff that largely organizes the worker's ideas and life. And, the same goes for the capitalist. Their morals are led by the quest for material enrichment, never the other way around. If a capitalist decides that their business decisions should follow only a pure moral urge to not exploit their workers, they will not be a capitalist for very long.

Life under the old Fordism appeared awesome and harmonious: a real model for the equilibrium a liberal economist would say is capitalism's natural state. The workers that build the goods buy the goods. The workers build pleasant communities around the factory. Mom-and-pop stores spring up to serve these communities, and they too got a slice of the fresh-baked Fordist pie. Migrants and Anglophone whites and blacks work together and sometimes even socialize together. They are content. They all drive Fords. They make more Fords. America buys Fords. Fords are distributed and sold throughout the nation, and then to the world! The cars become more sophisticated as the company competes for profit! Capitalism advances in victory! USA! USA!

Fordism looks like a great model. But, *only* through your capitalist viewfinder. If you look at it through Marx's spyglass, you can see that it's not sustainable, that it's just one part of a cycle destined to have crises and destined to end. Actually, you don't even need Marx here. All you need to do is look at a picture of the fallen city of Detroit, built in large part by Ford. This once grand place, where automobile workers were for a time so agreeably enslaved, is today in actual ruins.

*This* is the town that gave us that word, *Fordism*, to describe a kind of "I scratch your back" capitalism we like to believe can still exist: endless accord between generous entrepreneurs and grateful workers. This is a town in which beautiful stone monuments to America's can-do attitude stand. This was a town where the migrant who could not speak English or the black man who had never learned to read could make enough dough to not only have a nice life, but to have sufficient time to make beautiful culture. Forget the soaring ceilings and once-grand infrastructure of Detroit. The sign, for me, that it was once a marvelous place is the noise that it has made: Aretha. The White Stripes. John Lee Hooker. Derrick May. The MC5. Eminem. Not all of these artists lived in comfort, of course. But all of them lived in a city that was comfortable enough for long enough — it had the means to establish networks of support and recording studios that made the production of great culture possible.

We should mention here that Marx seriously dug the idea of finding time to produce great culture, or simply enjoying oneself. The guy loved to read a French novel, and often complained in his letters that he would much rather spend an afternoon in bed with Balzac than go on reading about this capitalism shit in the basement of the British Library. Marx loved the "spiritual and refined" things in life and there is, in my view, no smidgen of hypocrisy in this. Am I a champagne socialist? Too fucking right I am. What sort of person doesn't want to toast the end of class struggle with a nice glass of bubbles sourced from a wine-making collective? Marx was *all about* getting us more free time for culture, pleasure, and personal productivity. He gave up his own chance at leisure to ensure it. (Note, he *never* gave up drinking.)

So, yes: capitalism *can* have good pockets and periods, as it did in Detroit. This is absolutely not an un-Marxist thing to say. Capitalism has lifted some populations out of poverty. This, again, is not an un-Marxist thing to say. I will say, as a Marxist does, that such a time and place just doesn't last. It can't. Capitalism, like every system thus far tried in history, keeps moving. Sometimes it produces good results for some people. Sometimes it produces bad results for many. Always, this system that relies on taking a "surplus" from the worker (we'll explain this later on, promise) and making a profit will change, and reveal its strengths, ultimately its flaws.

Again, you can read about these contradictions in *Capital*. To understand them, you will need to get your head around Marx's labor theory of value, which holds that the profit made by capitalists is derived from human labor. As less human labor is needed, less profit can be made. I know that sounds strange. A really short and hopelessly basic version of all this is that capitalism, always on the edge of crisis, is destined to choke on its own surplus — see the tendency of the rate of profit (TRPF) to fall in Chapter 13 of Volume 3. Ugh. This stuff is hard. Let's keep talking about disasters we can see more easily and work our way up to this.

A few years after the financial crisis, Detroit, which no longer produces much great music, filed for bankruptcy — I mean *actually* filed for bankruptcy. This is not a metaphor, but a twenty-billion-dollar reality. Detroit's dilapidated civic buildings have since become the subject of a thousand paternalistic photography essays that white knowledge workers like me look at on their iPhones and say, "Oh, the municipal decay is both so beautiful and sad." Detroit's unemployment rate is staggering, and this has only fallen in recent years due to people fleeing the city and state statisticians continually finding new ways to define unemployment — in America, if you quit looking for work, or if you work for just a few hours, you are now no longer classified as unemployed. Although this hellhole now only sustains about 600,000 miserable people, there are more than three hundred homicides a year. Which is sixty more than the entire nation of Australia, with its still solvent population of 23 million, bears annually. Detroit is dying. Detroit is at war.

How the fuck did this happen? What produced this violence, one that has also claimed towns across Europe and is coming soon to a zip code near you? Are we going to say, "The people of Detroit are just bad"? No, we're not idealist fools, we have become historical materialists. So we will say that their *material* conditions had a great role in producing this disaster. A simpler way of saying this is that people with nothing get shitty and will often do what it takes to survive. You get a gun. You save yourself.

(You may, at this point, say that the answer to the problem of homicide in Detroit is gun control. I would not disagree that gun control is a good idea. But, I would urge you to think about two things when considering this. First, nothing, not even a gun, exists in a social vacuum. Second, imagine what it might be like to be a young poor black man in the United States. You face the very real possibility of death against a militarized police force whose hardware was once used in the war in Afghanistan. You face exclusion from any legitimate form of employment. Would you not, perhaps, also get yourself a gun? It's an arms race, baby. I include this observation not as part of our quick tour through capitalism and crisis, but just to remind you to be a good Marxist in general and look at the material circumstances in which people find themselves before coming up with a quick liberal solution like "gun control!" Which is, however noble and desirable, going to solve only a small part of the problem we describe.)

Many people, who still believe in the sweet dream of Fordist balance, use the term "crony capitalism" to explain a situation like

Detroit's. This is a way of saying that a few bad people made a few bad and greedy decisions. If people are good, the reasoning goes, then capitalism can be civilized. This is idealistic, in both senses of the word, as I explained it earlier. It's like saying, "A few bad apples spoil the bunch." A Marxist doesn't hold this view. A Marxist sees that you can't just trust people to be nice, or that you can't just go about blaming the bad ones. A Marxist wants a world where a certain amount of virtue *has* to happen because we've built it into the system. No "bad apple" theories for the Marxist. A Marxist does not believe that all people are truly marvelous and can be trusted to do good, but she does believe that the crate itself is rotten. (The apple crate is the capitalist mode of production, obvi. See. *Now* I'm using a metaphor.)

Marx and Engels used a lot of stirring metaphors in *The Communist Manifesto*, a pamphlet intended to reach the nineteenth-century working class. So let's go with a popular one of theirs: "What the bourgeoisie ... produces, above all, is its own grave-diggers." Capitalism, in other words, creates the conditions to kill itself. Just as I have my own dangerous genetic clumsiness, so does capitalism. Capitalism, as Marx saw it, has an internal contradiction, a barely visible button marked SELF-DESTRUCT. Let me try to break some important elements of this big Marxist idea down.

The gravediggers are us — paid and unpaid laborers alike. (Yes. You're still a worker bee for capitalism, even if unemployed. More on this later.) The suicidal bourgeoisie are the owners of the means of production, AKA the stuff — whether a factory or some proprietary piece of software — that we laborer gravediggers use to make other stuff. At times, the bourgeoisie creates much that is good for some of the gravediggers in the world. Or, in my current experience, much that is bearable. As we've said, *yes*, our lives are far easier to endure than most of those in the Global South. But, our lives ain't getting better. For Millennials in particular, life is getting worse. They don't call you guys a precariat for nothing.

Under current capitalism, I can buy cheap goods, including this cheap T-shirt, possibly made by a dead woman. Because her body is considered expendable and so very easy for capitalists to buy, this shirt is affordable to me and other workers in the West who live on a stagnant or declining wage. A wage that has stagnated or declined in recent decades precisely *because* this labor has been offshored to places where they let the factories fall down and drive the workers hard.

We can no longer afford to make these T-shirts in the West. Economists often call this the "Walmart effect." Most Western workers are now so badly paid, their clothes must be made by slaves to be affordable — and, sure, *technically* these seamstresses might not be slaves, but what else do you call someone who has the choice between hard labor or starvation? (Marx was always eager to point out, from his early twenties, that a legal guarantee of "freedom" is no real guarantee of anything at all. I am totally with him on this. I have never thought the right to free assembly is much use for someone tied all their waking hours to a production line.) These slave-made clothes are often placed on the shelves by the very people who buy them. The bourgeoisie talks about the "free market," but neither the people that make the shirt nor those that stock and buy the shirt are, in the Marxist view, anything close to free. A T-shirt is a harness with a worker at both ends.

Remember in the previous chapter we briefly looked at Donald Trump's persuasive election promise to restore manufacturing jobs in the United States? You remember the patriotic stuff he was going on with, right? No more China! No more Bangladesh! We'll charge those countries *so much* to sell their goods here, they won't send them anymore! We will make our own stuff. It will be tremendous! USA! USA! This sounded good to many unemployed and underemployed US voters who would have *loved* some honest work like making T-shirts to be sold in Walmart. But, this is a move Trump will not and cannot make.

Capitalism makes the Trump promise impossible — and who on Earth knows if the guy was actually too dumb to see that his promise was false? Whatever the case, it *is* false. If an American shirt is produced with American labor, its price will rise. American laborers, whose purchases are currently subsidized by the Walmart/slavery effect, will not be able to afford this shirt without a significant increase to their wages. The bourgeoisie, AKA the small group who own the means of production, has the following options under the Trump's supposed plan: (a) raise the price of the T-shirt, or (b) raise the wages of the American who made it, and also often the wages of the American who is going to sell it. Either way, the company will see their profits evaporate in this cycle of capitalism.

Trump's policies, often called protectionist, will not work. This is not to say that the United States *should* continue its program of globalization — as Clinton, who in 2012 called the Trans-Pacific Partnership "the gold standard," has long proposed, and as Trump will do in any case, despite his patriotic promises. What I am saying, along with Marx, is that we can neither sustain globalization *nor* go back to the old ways of local production, the latter of which being what both racist nationalists like Trump and soft-Left nationalists like Bernie Sanders were promising.

Hey, I am sorry to dis Bernie. He is a marvelous man, and what an important movement he revived. I have *nothing* but adoring things to say about Bernie's effectiveness as an educator. He explained the financial crisis to millions of interested people, most of whom were Millennials. But not even Bernie is so marvelous that he can "bring the jobs back."

Bringing the jobs back is a ridiculous promise to make. There *are* no Western jobs to bring back. This protectionism is bullshit. It is no longer the time of Ford, and we can't revive those old ways of doing capitalism when they are not profitable. Globalization, AKA global capitalism, is also bullshit — unless, of course, you can think of a good moral, or even rational, argument to keep the Global South in slavery until such time as this slavery ceases to be profitable to the West. Soon, there will be few jobs to "bring back" to those nations as well.

Workers in these slave nations are slowly being replaced by robots, and then denied even their current subsistence wages. They know it. They're not stupid. They know they may soon have nothing. What they will retain is the knowledge that Western governments and companies screwed them. To add to this crap, they live in regions disproportionately affected by climate change, and, in many cases, see US military and trade policy interventions close by.

We see the worrying way that some in the Global South are responding to globalization. You can shrug off radical Islamism as the idea of a deluded mind if you want. But you'd do well to remember that the way that some in the West responded to harsh conditions is with radical Trumpism. These are *terrible* reactions. They are *never* going to work. But this does not mean that the thing to which they are reacting is good. The capitalist mode of production is not currently working well. The political response, which is to continue doing capitalism in exactly the same way, is not working — people are voting against it. Global capitalism has become, as Marx predicted, disastrous. Our time may not be its endpoint, but it sure is one heck of a crisis.

As I told you a bajillion bloated words ago, Marxism is, in great part, an unflinching effort to understand the motion of capital. It is a method of thinking that allows us to understand crises of capitalism as they occur over time. It gives us the tools to create a new synthesis to address these crises. And this is why you have noticed a bunch of harpies, including myself, picking up the Marx lately and screaming, "HE TOTALLY WARNED YOU THIS WOULD HAPPEN!"

He really did. When I think about the T-shirt puzzle or the curious global production of an iPhone, I become convinced that Marx made a very good point about the suicidal tendency of capitalism. Can it really keep progressing all over the world like this without making most of us as shitty as the people of Detroit or Darfur?

Fordism gave the workers of Detroit cheap cars, wages to ensure that they could buy them, and time off so that they could go and create a rich music culture that would eventually give us techno. We can't go back to that, a period of such intense accumulation that it led to the Great Depression. (Cue the capitalist apologist: "What Depression?! No. That was not the failure of capitalism, but the work of a few bad apples!") Today, we have a new, strange post-Fordism: I, now in low-paid knowledge work, am no longer buying the T-shirt that I make, but instead the T-shirt made with the labor of some other poor fucker.

At this point, I'd like to remind you that the historical materialist doesn't fixate on that poor fucker. Just as we do not blame bad fuckers, we do not pity poor fuckers. Far better that we think of ourselves as a single class of workers. I reckon the "99 percent" label is a good one.

This solidarity is vital, and we'll discuss this often along the way. But, let me explain now some of the practical outcomes of refraining from pitying that individual worker.

First, the thought of, say, one dear lady losing her eyesight in unsafe conditions will only make us cry and render us *completely* useless to the revolution. Second, even if we personally adopt that worker — falsely presuming we could ever find her name — we haven't done anything to assist the peaceful suicide of capitalism, which is busy taking millions of other lives with it before it utters its last horrid and barbaric words. (I imagine these might be, "All I wanted to do was get the world to buy a Coke.")

And third, we must consider: how long will it be before *we* become those poor fuckers? Life in the West is no guarantee of safety. Just look to Detroit. Or shuttered towns in the United Kingdom and across continental Europe — places where much Trumpier versions of Trump are being elected. Can we *really* keep blaming the unemployed and the underemployed for their own misfortune? I don't think it's feasible to continue to tell a growing class of poors that they can pull themselves up by the bootstraps they are no longer employed to make.

What is built into this system is not only the enslavement of most of us to profit — that thing that can both revive and paralyze a poisonous idea like racism, depending on market conditions — but also capitalism's own end. Marx believes that capitalism will end, with or without a revolution. To be honest, he's pretty upbeat about it. Personally, when I think about how many ruptures it will cause, I'm not.

Capitalism is going to end! This might sound bonkers to you, but it makes perfect sense to anyone who has been a Marxist for more than a week. But, if this is the system in which you have lived in relative peace all your life, you might currently believe it to be the only system that works. There are, after all, plenty of people who will tell you that capitalism is the most natural thing in the world. We will be telling these people to go fuck themselves in several ways in following chapters. For the minute, let's stick with the imminent crisis.

If you want to read Marx's account of the inevitable crisis of capitalism, you'll find a big chunk of it in chapters 20 to 30 of Volume 1 of *Capital,* and also in Chapter 32. But to save you that right now, here are the SparkNotes.

The capitalist, to be successful, must grow her business. If she does not grow her business, another business will grow large enough to eat her business whole. The weak and the small are consumed by the strong and the big, which leads to a concentration of capital in the hands of a few. Capital becomes centralized. Stasis and equality are not possible within a business or system that depends on growing profits, and so we have as much hope of returning our national economies to Fordism as we do of ramming an ocean of toothpaste back into a single empty tube. The Ford company cannot go backwards to replicate its briefly harmonious period of growth and opportunity for its workers (although, interestingly, Ford does pretend that it still has this locally focused ethos in its public communications). Capitalist economies and firms move ahead, fuelled also, and entirely, by the search for profit. Capitalism mutates, or "evolves," if you prefer. Either way, as it ages, it acquires new postures and appetites.

As Marx relays in Chapter 14 of Volume 3 of *Capital,* capitalism, unlike the modes of production that came before, can adapt and survive downturns through the use of things like foreign labor power, cheapened commodities and other counteracting influences. But — and this is the important thing for Marx and what sets him apart from the classical thinking that still, in essence, sets policy for most economies in the world, and lending organizations like the World Bank and the IMF — he knew that capitalism was a fundamentally unstable system. Set aside, again, that it is also exploitative or immoral. Marx argues that it has a tendency, over time, to exhaust itself.

Okay. Let's keep looking at cars.

After Fordism ceased to be profitable, we began to do things the Toyota way. Toyotism — I promise it's an actual word that people use with their human mouths — means keeping production very "fluid." This means no longer making a car in anticipation of consumer demand, but using a "just in time" system of manufacturing and distribution, in which a laborer clicks the thing together only after someone commits to buy it. This means that workers are no longer on the assembly line working in reliable conditions, but called in when needed. These unstable working conditions did not produce warm and creative communities, like early Detroit. They probably *did* make available some of that supercharged Japanese speed I've read about.

Marx says that a firm's search for profit must lead it to develop new techniques to stay competitive. It was once the case that this meant treating your workers well. It now means that you put them on zero-hour contracts, leaving them uncertain if they'll be able to pay their bills this week. Perhaps this is the way you work? This is the way that I now work — I haven't had a salary in years because I, apparently, am an "entrepreneur." Plenty of us work in this insecure way, which we are often encouraged to think of as exciting and innovative. Because *what* could be more inspiring than racking up massive personal debt and feeling uncertain in your job? *Oh, every day I respond to the thrill of income instability with wonderful life hacks, mindfulness training, and Kundalini yoga. I'm so agile!*

I want to make the point here that your boss, even if they are an asshole, is not doing this stuff to you only because they are an asshole. They don't necessarily think "How shall I make Helen feel crappy today?" And, even if they do think that way, they are doing it because this is what the unsustainable, always growing system of capitalism demands. We can't really have personal morals around work when the work itself is arranged by capitalism, which is a system, ergo not a human with morals.

When Toyota started their business model in the 1960s, they didn't do it because they were assholes. When Ford started his in the early twentieth century, he didn't do it because he was a sweetheart. Both these companies, which remain the most money-spinning car manufacturers in the world, did it for the same reason: profit. Profit. This is the only "morality" of capitalism.

New techniques of employment are not decided by workers. They may not even be preferred by your manager. You are a part-time, casual, or contract employee not because your boss doesn't like you enough to give you holidays, but because that is what the mode of production, capitalism, finds most profitable. The outlets to which I sell my labor don't pay me piecework rates because they hate me — I am fortunate to enjoy friendly relations with my "clients," which is to say, the people who buy my labor commodity — but because that is what the mode of production currently demands. They are good people who apologize weekly for the low wages they pay me. I know that they must profit from my labor in order to stay in business. This "gig economy" — the casual, part-time and contract jobs that have replaced the former full-time labor economy — is one of capitalism's new self-preserving techniques.

As Marx says in *Capital* (if I had a dollar for every time I've been ejected from a dinner table for using *that* phrase, I probably wouldn't hate capitalism so much), new technologies will also be devised along with these new techniques. As new machines — from the combine harvester to the bulldozer to the factory robot — are activated, the ways in which a worker can earn a wage shifts. And the way in which a capitalist can maintain her business moves toward its end. Both new technologies, such as the 3D printer, and new techniques, such as offshoring labor, throw many out of a job. These also eventually destroy the capitalists who oversee the creation of these new technologies. The Marxist thinking goes: human labor is the source of all profit. The surplus, or the hours you work that produce more money than you are paid, is what produces profit. If a firm gets rid of human labor and replaces it with machines, which a firm actually *must* do to stay profitable in the short term, then profit dwindles over time. YES. This is hard to get your head around. Stick with me here. If we both get 'round to understanding Marx's TRPF, we will be able to impress sexy Marxists by throwing it into casual conversation. But these machines can't be uninvented.

Marx, who was writing at the time of the Industrial Revolution, did say that capitalism would tend, for a time, to create new industries and new jobs in the dominant economies. He also said that it was not always profitable to replace human labor with that of machines. Sometimes, he observed, it was cheaper to use an exploited English worker to break stones than the stone-breaking machines invented in the then fast-growing economy of the United States. But, eventually, he claimed, the process of innovation would speed up so much that human labor would no longer be needed in large numbers.

As each company succeeded in getting the innovation edge over the other, as they *must* to survive and make a profit, a tiny minority of very rich capitalists would emerge. And even these guys would eventually be undone by their own innovation. If you have a business that no longer requires human labor, which you must in order to beat the other guy, what you eventually have is a business that can no longer have growth but will instead decline.

Think of our worker who made my cheap T-shirt. The capitalist can profit from her. He can buy her labor for a low cost every day. He extracts value from her. She grows his profits in a way that a machine never can. He buys the machine just once. He buys her and extracts value from her many times. It is her living labor that enables him to grow.

I know it seems whacko. You'd think "Well, isn't it profitable to save on labor costs?" Well. Yes and no and sometimes.

Before we have a look at the very irritating TRPF, let's just remember the Walmart effect above. That's when your goods must be made at a cost low enough that workers can afford them. If there are fewer workers, then there are fewer people to buy shit.

Some big business owners and investors have newly realized that there are problems served up by the work robot. This is why the chief of Tesla, Elon Musk, is proposing something called Universal Basic Income be paid to all US citizens by the government — that's a chunk of money paid to everyone. Titans like Musk have innovated so much, they no longer need workers. Musk is a pretty bright guy and can see that the future for workers is dark. He knows that he needs the money previously provided by wages to stay in business. So now, he is petitioning the state to give the people money so they can give him money. Musk is a clever dude, but is unable, thanks to "ideology," which we'll look at in Chapter 3, to see the contradiction here. Who will pay the taxes that will pay people not to work? Elon? I'm guessing not.

On to TRPF and how new tech that replaces workers can tend to reduce profit. The first firm that invests in new labor-saving machinery can offer their goods to market at a discount rate. But then, all firms start to use this labor-saving tech — they must in order to stay competitive. You don't make a shirt with the labor of people for ten bucks when you can make it for five with a machine. The market advantage is immediately lost when all firms use this new device. The investment advantage the firm made in tech will be eventually lost.

A firm can profit better from what Marx calls the *variable* capital of human labor. Over time, a firm will not profit from the *constant* capital of a tool or a machine. A firm's one-time-only payment for a labor-saving device, constant capital, will bring in a profit for a while. A firm's payment for the variable capital of human labor would continue to bring in a profit for a longer period. One firm starts making cheapo drills, blenders, or sex robots with work robots? Next, all the firms do.

It is usually profitable to save on labor. It is always necessary to create new labor-saving tech. Marx observed all this stuff, and predicted a time when the power of capitalists would far exceed that ever held by any feudal lord or ancient slave-master. Just a few people would own all the capital. At different times many people would find themselves without work, replaced by new technology. Wealth would centralize. People would get mighty pissed off.

He *told* us this would happen. There are eight guys who now own more wealth than the poorest half of the planet. *Eight* guys.

You have close to a one-in-a-billion chance of joining the new slave-master class. These guys all run businesses, or own interests in businesses, that have a reduced need for labor.

Number one on the rich list, for example, is Jeff Bezos. This guy still employs laborers in his Amazon warehouses, but given that these troublesome humans are wont to complain about things like low pay, long hours, strip searches, and falling over in the heat of his warehouses, he'll eventually replace them with robots. In late 2016, Bezos opened his pilot no-human supermarket in Seattle, called Amazon Go. Swipe your phone and walk into the ghost store. Make a purchase direct from the shelves. Wave goodbye to retail as we know it, currently the largest employment sector in the West.

For Bezos, like Ford before him, morals are shaped by his wealth. Just as Ford decided not to act like a racist when it suited his business, Bezos made a moral about-face, too. Before he was in the Top Eight, Bezos was a "libertarian" who gave substantial donations to the Reason Foundation, a pro "freedom of speech" think tank that opposed Obamacare and any efforts by any government to "intervene" in anything, but mostly in the wealth of the rich and the death of the poor.

Bezos then purchased a newspaper. In the *Washington Post* we can see the new "morals" of this billionaire in black and white: Obama was now his guy. The paper supported Hillary Clinton unstintingly throughout the US election, including in the primaries when it took the piss out of Bernie Sanders. It continues a campaign to discredit Donald Trump, who had suggested that Bezos should be paying more tax, repeatedly claiming that "the Russians" had "hacked the election" — we hear this a lot because many refuse to believe that the people voted against Clinton's traditional capitalism themselves. Bezos, a one-time libertarian, has decried WikiLeaks, and his paper continues to publish personal attacks on Julian Assange. Assange is still accused of "hacking the election," merely by publishing the speeches Clinton made to Wall Street. By publishing the spoken truth. The Bezos Foundation has donated to the Clinton Foundation. The Clinton-led state department had funded Amazon directly. A capitalist's morals are entirely informed by profit. These become our morals.

The moral of the non-moral story is: if you want to learn about a capitalist's morals, follow his money.

If you want to learn about the inevitable decline of capitalism, and the morals that sustain it, read Marx.

A person enamored of capitalism will tell you that the market *always* finds a way (even though the market has never found a "way" to feed all the workers of the world throughout their lives). "Sure," they say, "we may be replaced by new technologies and techniques, but there will always be more growth and emerging industries!"

In certain places and for a short time Marx predicted this would be true — capitalism would be able to sustain itself (although even in economies like the United States and Australia, where a large middle class prospered for decades, there were always have-nots, often identifiable by their gender or the color of their skin). The view that the market will always magically balance itself has been discredited by what we see before us today: dilapidated Western cities, mass starvation in the Global South, kids with postgrad degrees in biotech driving Ubers. These things didn't happen overnight. They did, however, happen.

Forty years of growing wealth inequality is not, as liberal economists will say, a "market correction." It's an intergenerational disaster, whose shape was sketched by Marx, and whose problems are now being described by more centrist economists such as Thomas Piketty, who made world headlines with his "r > g" formula in the bestselling book *Capital in the Twenty-First Century.*

Piketty is not a Marxist, but this doesn't mean we shouldn't dismiss his famous "r > g." This means that "r," which is the rate of return on capital — the money or assets that you use, if you're a rich fucker, to make more money — exceeds "g," which is the rate of an economy's growth. Basically, it means "Wealth grows faster than the economy." or, if you prefer, "Learn to drive an Uber, and hope that it's a few years before that massively valued company replaces you with a driverless car."

If you personally enjoy a nice and secure life, I do not ask you to feel any guilt. I wish that material comfort for you just as I wish it for all people. *Nobody* should spend twelve hours driving or sewing, unless they happen to really fancy doing so one Tuesday.

This is what a Marxist wants: for everyone to have a nice bed and contentment and access to the abundance and technology we workers have all built. The fact is, most people in the world *don't* have anything like it. Most people in the world have *never* had it under capitalism. Even those of us who are holding on to the remnants of our wealth can sense it disappearing fast. The abundance that capitalism has created is now available only to a few.

Mass unemployment and underemployment is already occurring — and, please, before you claim that unemployment remains at the ideal "five percent" in Western nations, have a look at how the way that unemployment is defined has changed. Even the Reserve Bank of Australia publicly stated in 2016 and again in early 2017 that there might be something a *little* unhelpful in those numbers. The "evidence" is made to fit the policy, and rarely the other way around.

This is also true for World Bank data on poverty. Those guys change their criteria for poverty about as often as Apple upgrades its OS. Do you think there might be a reason that people at the United Nations have started using "happiness" as a measure for a nation's wealth, rather than boring old things like purchasing power? This strikes me as the most racist Western crap. It's like your white hippie uncle who vacations in Bali and comes back to report, "Those people might not have much, but they seem so happy!" Yeah, whatever you need to tell yourself to justify hiring an impoverished sex worker for three dollars, Unc. We are creatures with material needs. I do not believe that there is any nation so spiritually advanced it can overcome the need for clean water, or the revulsion for my uncle. Happiness, my ass.

(N.B. Not to "judge" sex work. The Marxist sees this labor as indistinct from any other. You're selling your body and mind for profit just like the rest of the working class.)

What rising unemployment and underemployment mean for us in the West are several shitty things. First, and most obviously, we may soon be out of a job, depressed and starving. Second, the increasing scarcity of work means that employers have the whip hand: if there is, as Engels put it, a "reserve army of the unemployed," then employers are freer to pay desperate workers shitty wages and make unreasonable demands. Third, a big "reserve army of the unemployed" will not, in the end, be great for most capitalists.

Perhaps the problem inherent in this inevitable capitalist accident has already occurred to you in your daily life: if I don't have any money, and my friends don't have any money, how is anyone going to take the money I don't have? If fewer of us have money to buy the goods and services produced by machines, fewer goods and services will be bought. If more and more of us are living in some version of Detroit, where the supermarkets are shuttered, there will be fewer companies making profit, whose profits are, in any case, doomed to fail by the larger factors that cycle under consumption. There will continue to be a greater and greater accumulation of wealth by the few. Then, of course, there will be significantly reduced motivation to drive the technological innovation on which so many arguments for the excellence of capitalism depend.

Without a revolutionary change in the way we do things and own things, these can-do capitalists are just going to keep digging their own graves, and — despite Marx's certainty that we would all dance at capitalism's wake — ours, too.

Politicians say that capitalism will adapt. They say, "Uber is so innovative and convenient!" until they're Clinton-blue in the face, but they can't continue to shy away from Uber's future, which we now look to as a guide to the future of capitalism.

Currently, Uber — valued at the time of writing at US$65 billion — which began piloting a program of driverless cars in Pittsburgh in 2016, has since expanded to other cities. They don't make a secret of the fact that this is their future business model. I mean, sure, the board says stuff like, "Uber is helping millions of people find flexible work!" in releases to the general press. But the story they tell financial publications is rather different.

Uber is currently making no profit at all, and just ride-sharing high on the erections of Silicon Valley venture capitalists. What happens when this immense company rolls its little smart cars further afield than Pittsburgh, now free of the annoying driver eating away at their profit? All those Uber jobs go. And, in the meantime, Uber has knocked out all competitors through its low fares. Uber will then hike its prices. Again, this is not because Uber was run by dicks — although Uber was run by a guy who seems like a complete dick — but just because profit is what capitalism must seek. Capitalism is a system, not a moral beast. We Marxists do not ask it moral questions we know that it is simply not capable of addressing. You may as well ask a lump of coal, "Why do you pollute so?"

I have spoken with many Uber drivers about the driverless pilot program. The guys who came to Australia from UNHCR camps are resigned to the whole thing. Mohammed (Uber five-star rating) said it didn't surprise him, as his life had often been a case of running from one place to the next. Other guys from Western nations say that the driverless car thing will *never* happen. Nobody will trust these new vehicles, they say. I tell them that our great-great-great-grandparents once said that about Ford's Model T. When Horace Rackham, a Ford investor, asked for financial guidance from a prominent Michigan banker in 1903, he was told, "The horse is here to stay, but the automobile is only a novelty — a fad."

As I enjoy my cheap rides and depressing revolutionary conversations with drivers, I wonder who is going to be able to afford an Uber in twenty years. I can't see Uber remaining available to the masses. Probably guys who work at places like Uber will use Uber. Lawyers who spend their days figuring out elaborate ways for Uber not to pay tax will do two things as they ride around in their driverless Ubers. First, they will introduce the word *Uberism* to business schools. Second, they will accidentally push us towards the endpoint of Marx's argument. Capitalism will fail so colossally to meet the needs of the many that the many will get the shits.

I also wonder who will innovate when the wealth is held completely by so few. We've seen how capitalists change their morals when it suits their profit. There is no reason to expect they'll innovate just for love alone. Competition creates innovation. There is now little competition.

Through technology, Uber does away with its profit-gobbling workers. It now dominates the transport market. Why, in the name of Tesla, would it bother to spend money on further innovation?

The new ride-sharing middle class will be a tiny group of happy suits, only briefly troubled when they wonder why no one makes good music anymore. (Remember Detroit?) The ruling class will be an even tinier group, recognizable by their "hip" T-shirts — perhaps you have noticed how the Silicon Valley bourgeoisie likes to dress in the clothes of a rebel. These guys are regular Che Guevaras. The majority of us will be unemployed, perhaps thirty percent of us working in those low-paid jobs where humans cannot yet be viably or profitably replaced. Agriculture, manufacturing, transport, construction, retail, mining, and logistics will be work chiefly done by machines. (The Western jobs likely to remain, curiously, will be those traditionally performed by women. What happens then is anybody's guess. Perhaps low-paid health care work will suddenly become a butch thing to do. Perhaps men will start blaming pushy women for their poverty. Either way, my money's on a gender-based Hunger Games if we don't end up with a revolutionary alternative.)

Marx predicted this scenario. He predicted that the decline of the middle class, and the concentrated wealth of the bourgeoisie, would produce great anger. What happens when you throw a formerly well-to-do capitalist or middle-class success in with the rest of us? We are a class always increasing in number, he said. We are now joined by the formerly elite, the urbanized, the newly pissed off. And now, "All that is solid melts into air, all that is holy is profaned, and man is at last compelled to face with sober senses his real conditions of life, and his relations with his kind."

In other words, the many cranky people just kicked out of the nice bathroom have become part of our class. Their poverty, which is so new, makes even less sense to them than it does to us. They want to smash shit up.

Shit is going to get smashed. In the very near future, a bunch of angry former elites are those likely to smash shit hardest, and, given their insider knowledge, with greatest precision. They know where the really valuable stuff is hidden.

We welcome you, comrades. Though we do want you to know that we've been at this for a while, and would kindly ask that you put away the semiautomatic you received as part of your quarterly performance bonus. The Marxist would prefer to do this as nicely and as safely as possible. We do this with solidarity. We do this with *thought*.

Thought is difficult. It is intellectually difficult; it is difficult to understand how capitalist enterprise, which has depended for its growth on the exploitation of human labor, fails as human labor is replaced. It is emotionally difficult; it is difficult to think of the lady that made my T-shirt. Nonetheless, what we all *must* bear is thought. We must now examine an unsustainable system that profits from human destitution. We must say, as Marx said, that the only way to our collective freedom is through our true collective ownership of this world, with all its machines.

We must take it. It is, and always has been, ours to take. The innovative machines built by the labor of our comrades. Let's take it back. The profitable people dumped in private prisons serving sentences for minor crimes. Let's take them back. The lives of the women at the Rana Plaza disaster. We can't take them back, but what we can take back is the lives of their daughters. We *can* give freedom, to each and to all.

We're in this together. Those of us who work for money are in it. Those of us who keep wages down through our unemployed status are in it. Those of us who care for others are in it. We are all, save for the one percent of the one percent, *in* this, and if you weren't tipped off by the whole "one percent of the one percent" percentage, here's the thing: there are *way* more of us than there are of them.

What will they say if we demand our stuff back? How will they counter our claim that freedom belongs to each, as it does to all? How will they argue with the truth that most of us are living in, or are shortly to encounter, a bucket of capitalist waste?

I guess they could just say, "No, you're quite wrong." They could try to divide us by race, faith, sexuality, and gender. They *will* do that. Be ready for this divisive nonsense when you start to ask your questions. Be ready for them to keep the totalizing force of capital alive by telling us that we're not *all* in this together.

# 3

---

## "That Feeling When" You Totally Thought You Were Doing That, But You Were Totally Doing Something Else! "OMG"! Frown Face!

---

f you and I ever meet, comrade, demand from me the reward of an awkward hug and a flute of socialist champagne. Frankly, you deserve both, having made it this far. You've pushed your way through an account of something with a ten-buck name like "historical materialism," you now know a little of the fatal tendencies of capital accumulation and you *didn't even do it for work or school*. Heck, you may have even *paid* for this book — and I'm sorry about that, but, like you, I am a worker coerced by the conditions of the market. "Girl's gotta eat," as Marx said in *Theories of Surplus Value*.

Okay. He doesn't say this anywhere, precisely. But, I'm taking the opportunity to remind you *again*: the Marxist believes that the way our material needs are met largely informs the way our societies are organized and understood. *Remember*: the superstructure and the base. The idea and the material. They interweave. It's NOT just bad ideas that produce bad lives. The opposite is even more true.

Seriously, though, comrade. *Thanks*. I know there are greater pleasures available to you than me and Marx, and I *do* understand that you have already endured quite a bit of pain. This Marxism stuff isn't easy. So, I sincerely wish I could say that from this point our journey toward freedom, for each and for all, will be nothing but a cakewalk. But that would be a fib, as I am about to thwack you with one of the most potentially troubling Marxist ideas. Let's say "Hey" to "ideology."

In an intellectual sense, you probably won't find the notion of ideology very troubling to understand at all — it's pretty easy and I'll happily bet you already get it, even before having it explained. *Emotionally*, however, you may find it very challenging, as I have myself. To accept the Marxist idea of ideology is, in part, to accept that we need to individually un-fuck ourselves from the inside. Ideology is the political unconscious. Undoing this can sometimes be a painful therapy.

The word *ideology* is not used by a Marxist in the way it generally is. Many people today use it to describe their conscious belief system.

You might say, "I have a feminist ideology." You won't ever hear a Marxist, however feminist they are, say this. For us, "ideology" describes a set of unconscious beliefs; specifically those that exist to uphold the way in which we currently organize our political economies.

Ideology was used prior to Marx to mean a self-identified set of beliefs, and it is widely used that way today once more. I don't want to make some purist case for language use here. But, given that Marx and Engels used it to mean a very specific thing, chiefly in *The German Ideology*, it's just easier if I use it in that specific way, too. I don't want other comrades laughing at you as you storm the Winter Palace screaming, "This is my ideology!" They'll be all "lol wot!" Or, worse, they'll confuse you for a capitalist.

Marx had this idea that capitalism dug its own defences deep into our minds. *This* is what he means by ideology. Now, this might sound crazy. What does he mean that I don't *know* what I think? That the exchange of commodities influences my innermost thoughts?! But this is only until you remember that Sigmund Freud came up with a very similar idea just a few decades later, and that his is one that continues to powerfully inform Western thought. You probably don't have much difficulty believing that you have certain emotional beliefs or urges that are somehow concealed from your conscious mind.

The Freudian "superego" describes that semi-conscious part of our minds that internalizes dominant morals, *even* those that may not have been directly communicated to us. We sometimes call this our conscience, and it's the thing that shrieks, for example, "Masturbation is filthy and wrong!" even if we have never heard such a thing said to us in all our lives.

How did we learn that having a good old tug is considered sinful, even if no one has explicitly issued us with any kind of anti-fapping decree? How did some of us embed in our heads the idea that this kind of sexual pleasure is the darkest work of Satan? There are plenty of people who feel shame, even in the Western present, at the point of climax. And, jeez, I'm certain that Oprah has produced at least a dozen top-rating specials on the "benefits" of masturbation. Still, the idea persists in the hearts and pants of many, particularly older people, that pleasuring oneself is a vice. Clearly, it's not — I personally consider it little more than a pleasant way to kill forty-five seconds. But the fact that coming can come for some with painful guilt is a proof of the fact that dumb ideas, often unspoken, can settle in our minds and afflict our bodies. They settled in so many bodies and minds so firmly once that they served to preserve the dominant sexual order — in this case, one which demanded that the seed of men be spilled only for the purposes of making babies and that women never get a hold of this whole self-pleasure idea lest they start enjoying themselves and decide to stop caring for babies and men.

It is, if you like, an *ideology* that masturbation is bad — not the capitalist ideology that Marx writes about, but an ideology all the same. We have had certain subtle ideological tools for communicating this masturbation fact — and, in one sense, it is a "fact," as well as an ideology, that masturbation is *bad*. It was bad for the once socially desired relations between husband and wife — it was, as they say in Silicon Valley, a disruption. It is also a "fact" that masturbation can come to be good, while also remaining a destructive ideology. You know all those apparently feminist articles that say that it's GREAT for women to masturbate? These are also ideological. Which is to say, in the Marxist sense, they are articles that serve the interests of the ruling class.

When midcentury mothers referred to their daughters' sex organs only by noting their dark absence — "down there" — they communicated that it was forbidden territory. When our mass-media mothers of the present day, like Oprah Winfrey, laugh at the olden times where our own vaginas appeared to us as the end of the flat world on an old map marked "There be dragons!" they communicate a new kind of ideological "fact."

Old mothers said that pleasure was bad for the order of the world. They were right. New mothers say that pleasure is good for the order of the world. They are also right. The new ideology, the thing that holds up dominant order, often encourages women to masturbate. It's good for your productivity, they say. It's good for your happiness and your skin! It makes you *feel* good. What's more important than feeling good? Well, I'm so glad you asked me that, Oprah. In my view, it is better, at times, to feel angry. After all, this anger may help me smash capitalism.

I have seen and read so many instructions to masturbate in recent years, I have largely given up masturbating. I do not wish to have my own physical desire pressed into the service of either good housekeeping or productive, happy female work. Whether I am being told to *refrain* from masturbation lest I disturb the dominant order or to *embrace* masturbation lest I disturb the dominant order, I resent the intrusion of ideology into my vagina.

For a while, I wondered what Freud would have thought of an age that wasn't merely permissive about unleashing female desire, but positively oppressive and *repressive* in its attempts to make all of us masturbate a lot — on UK TV, one of the networks even has an annual Wank Week, much of whose content is specifically aimed at my abused clitoris.

What *would* Freud have said? The Freudian Marxist, Theodor Adorno, comes close to giving us an answer. He said that our age was one of "psychoanalysis in reverse." I really love that description, and I think it helps us understand the nature of what Marx and other Marxists mean when they use the word *ideology*.

Ideology is a mystification, but not necessarily a lie. It conceals a truth about the dominant order inside itself. The reality, in the case of female masturbation, is that it is a thing some are able to do. The mystification of this reality has been that it is *bad* and is now, more commonly, that it is *good*.

Psychoanalysis, a study that has been hybridized by many Marxists including Adorno, Louis Althusser, and mutant brat Slavoj Žižek, seeks to get to the truth between consciousness and being. It might analyze people, or entire populations, with this goal in mind. It seeks a language for the way we conscious beings mystify our being. Through techniques like word association, dream analysis, or listening for our slips in speech, it looks for the code to what we have repressed.

Just as I can embed the message "masturbation is bad" deep within my mind, I can do the same with "masturbation is good." Dr. Freud himself could have not imagined a time where women would be saying the latter nonstop on TV shows for aspirational working girls who crave that post-fap glow. Ideology continues its work of mystification and gets into our pants anyhow with the reverse of the old masturbation message. Ergo, I find that Oprah has really ruined one of my favorite hobbies with her "psychoanalysis in reverse." Oprah's is a false openness. It claims to open everything up but, in so doing, still suggests a prohibition: there's something wrong with you if you don't masturbate.

This is the thing about ideology. The message and the means of its conveyance can change. We only know it to be ideology when we can *finally* see that it makes us servants of the dominant order.

To continue with masturbation, an activity I clearly miss, let's think about the ways in which it was otherwise controlled. We've covered the ideological methods of controlling it, where a girl would learn that "down there" lay dragons or a boy might hear that he'd be marked by blindness. In reading accounts of Victorian era anti-masturbation methods, we learn what happened to middle-class fappers when the soft power of ideology did not work. There were young boys who had anti-masturbatory devices applied to their genitals at night and adult men of the professional class were known to apply their own medically prescribed safeguards. You can even go and see some of these instruments of torture in London's Victoria and Albert Museum. Although these apparatuses were inspired by ideology, we can't call a metal thing on your cock pure ideology. *That* is not a mystification. When the mystification doesn't work to control you, that's when they bring in the serious hardware.

You can think about the control of certain groups of people in this way, too. Once, black people in the United States were held in chains and Aboriginal people in Australia were held in missions in order to steal, respectively, their labor and their land. Liberalism eventually removed these constraints, and replaced them with the invisible bonds of ideology, and these worked for a while to maintain the illusion of freedom — remember, Aboriginal land was never returned and black labor remains the cheapest in the United States. Racist ideology began to fail as a means of control and today again we see black people incarcerated and murdered by US police, and Aboriginal people subject to incarceration and programs of state control. These physical controls, such as the use of military and surveillance techniques — what Althusser would call "State Ideological Apparatuses" — are combined with softer forms of ideological control, such as the very common and peculiar insistence that black people are acting "like victims" when they point to the (very real and material) fact of their own victimhood.

I'd best be honest here and say that not all Marxists will hold fully with this description of ideology. If you've already done a little time with Karl, you may know that ideology was the preoccupation only of the younger man. You might even know that my decision to write an entire chapter on ideology would be, for some, quite questionable. Yeah, you're right. There *are* important scholars who argue that Marx's later and most important work *Capital* does away with the concept of ideology and replaces it with the mystified nature of the commodity — that three-dollar T-shirt from Dhaka that contains so many secrets. Who made it? Is she still alive? Who packed it, and who owned the cotton? Why do they own so much cotton when others have nothing? These are just some of the questions we rarely let the T-shirt ask us. If we did allow ourselves to be fully connected to the way the T-shirt was made, then profit may start to unravel.

But, ARGH, this is some heavy shit that takes us right to one of the old guy's most challenging concepts. The older Marx explains to us how the commodity, the thing made by labor, comes to deaden our relationship with ourselves and each other and our world. The space between being and consciousness is mystified by the things that we can buy, the things many of us *must* buy in order to survive. Frankly, Section 4 of Chapter 1 of Volume 1 of *Capital* is a total mind fuck. Read it and reread it, but know it will screw with you intellectually *and* emotionally. I have promised to fuck with you only *emotionally* right now, so I intend to honor only *that* cruel vow.

Ideology, like Freud's superego, remains a really useful way of understanding things. If you become a studious Marxist, you might soon decide to abandon this relatively simple concept of a political unconscious in favor of a more complex understanding. Even so, you'll retain the belief that people can be very deeply deluded about capitalism, or that they can, after some effort and experience, become what you youngsters call "woke," or what we old Marxists call "class conscious."

Before we can seize the means of production, transform the mode of production and then enjoy hours of freedom filled with both meaningful and mindless human activity — this may include authoring an open-source gardening almanac or having a fap — we must be conscious of our class. Each Marxist must identify her place within a political economy to have the hope of transforming it for all.

If you are a progressive person, you might not be altogether unfamiliar with the process of an internal political audit. You might have previously found that you have carried racist, sexist, or homophobic ideas inside you. You might have, very honorably, addressed these and told yourself to remain vigilant in case you ever start thinking of brown people as "deeply spiritual," women as "very nurturing," or queer people as "great fun." You recognize that even an upbeat form of bigotry can act to enforce the behavior of others. And, what sort of shithead wants to do that?

We can call all these forms of bigotry "ideological." Which is to say, they each, if unexamined, function very efficiently to reinforce dominant power structures. The experience of bearing such ideology is individual and unconscious. The effect of it is often collective — lots of white people think brown people are "deeply spiritual" or somehow stuck in an ancestral past — and often experienced very consciously by those to whom it is unconsciously applied. If you have been on the wrong end of someone's unconscious bigotry, you often fucking know about it, even if it's tricky to explain.

Say you're a transperson having a chat with a cisperson and you can tell by their language and gestures that they think you are not trans, just "confused." This is their perspective, and it informs their attitude to you utterly. Even if you're not talking about anything to do with gender or sexuality at all — not that you *are* confused by these things because as a transperson, you've thought about them *way* more than most — they still think you're "confused." They may speak to you slowly, or display a visible exertion when required to use the pronoun you have said that you prefer. They might just treat you like a child, because they couldn't possibly think that a *rational adult* would transition. They're not asking you rude questions about your genitals or calling you a freak, but their concealed assumptions present themselves quite nakedly to you. It's a vibe. Which is a very difficult thing to wrestle with, or to point out to others.

There's some correspondence I like very much, written by Martin Luther King Jr. to his fellow black clergymen while he was behind bars in 1963. In *Letter from a Birmingham Jail*, he describes the frustrations of ideology well:

> I must confess that over the past few years I have been gravely disappointed with the white moderate. I have almost reached the regrettable conclusion that the Negro's great stumbling block in his stride toward freedom is not … the Ku Klux Klanner, but the white moderate, who is more devoted to "order" than to

justice … who constantly says: "I agree with you in the goal you seek, but I cannot agree with your methods of direct action"; who paternalistically believes he can set the timetable for another man's freedom; who lives by a mythical concept of time and who constantly advises the Negro to wait for a "more convenient season." Shallow understanding from people of good will is more frustrating than absolute misunderstanding from people of ill will. Lukewarm acceptance is much more bewildering than outright rejection.

It's interesting to note here that King was treated very badly on this occasion in jail and had been arrested for protesting — ostensibly, his inalienable right. Even amid all this crude KKK-style brutality, he still found the words to say what needed to be said: it's the power you cannot easily identify that's the most devastating. The hardware or the weapons can crush you. The police can beat you. But, yes, *even* for a Marxist, the idea, not the material reality, can be the most brutal. I am making the case again here that there is more unity between thought and being, or the superstructure and the base, in Marxist thought than is commonly understood.

Ideology, which is often expressed in a naive spirit of generosity, brings with it particular frustration. Out-and-out hatred is tough to confront, of course. But I have wondered at times whether I find it more tolerable to be called, as I sometimes am on the internet, a "rabid fat commie whore" than the more frequent and more ideological "insensitive." I know that the latter is actually a quite sexist and capitalist thing to say, and that people mean that it is unfeminine to talk about economics rather than feelings. This feels to me like psychoanalysis in reverse. How *dare* you try to open me up falsely with your ideological half-truth! How dare you expect that a woman should talk only about the hard time *she* had, rather than the hard time *everyone* is having?

"Shallow understanding from people of good will is more frustrating than absolute misunderstanding from people of ill will." It's a great thing for white people to be told, right? The next time you, if white, are tempted to join in an afternoon of shaming an unabashed racist on the internet, reflect that "the white moderate who paternalistically believes *he* can set the timetable for another man's freedom" might be a more formidable enemy to justice than the racist.

I know there is one word white people can utter to diminish a black or a brown person in an instant. I know that I will be likely to act when I hear it. As a Marxist, though, I believe in the relative futility of my act. I am not being brave or useful — *especially* if I offer my protest before giving the person who bore the terrible insult a chance to respond. If I'm honest, my protest serves *me* in this case. *Oh, Helen, you're just so compassionate and you're saving the world, one brown person at a time!* This is, in fact, ideology. To believe that I can act alone to achieve significant historical change is some grade-A liberal bullshit. I am calling "call out" culture ideological.

It is, of course, very useful for me, and any Marxist, to be able to observe the "fact" behind the mystification of ideology. We call it out in ourselves, and we may do so in good faith to our comrades. But we don't think that going clear, Scientology style, is an end in itself. We never think we have the individual power to transform history.

We also think about where and when to rip off the veil of mystification so that others may see it. There are plenty of people committed to social justice who enthusiastically rip off veils that have long been thrown by history to the ground. There's little point in me attacking something that has already been widely revealed as a mystification. If I scream at a Pentecostal, "NO! Female masturbation is wonderful. In fact, I'm doing it now!" I simply uphold the newer ideology. Frankly, as a Marxist, I am more tempted to scream at Oprah. In fact, the next time she tells me that masturbation makes me a better worker bee, I think I will.

But were I to do so, in negating an idea already shown to be dead I would be reviving it. Not only would I breathe new life into the corpse of ideology, I would show myself to be what I have become: a politically correct adherent to empowering daytime TV. I would offer similar advice to any person considering protesting Milo Yiannopoulos. This overt racist, the kind Martin Luther King Jr. would prefer to the concealed one, grows richer and more influential with every disavowal from those white moderates he calls "cucks." In any case, Yiannopoulos, that hothouse weed, was largely transformed from a shit-posting nobody into a star because of the era's material conditions. You want people like Milo to go away? Sure, so do I. But what we must both work towards is a world that would not embrace him as a sassy guest at all. Jerks like Milo only become significant during an economic downturn. So, what are you waiting for, comrade? Let's stand together to change the mode of production. If only to shut Milo up.

(I am aware that Milo has shut up. But this was not due to the failure of capitalism, unfortunately. Instead, it was down to good old homophobia. Ideology allowed many people to tolerate him saying dreadful things about other people. When video surfaced of him talking about his own sexual preferences, though, that was, apparently, too much.)

There's naked glittery feral Milo-hate, and then there is the more formally attired ideological communication of it. Neither expression is desirable, of course. But there is a case to be made that bad views clad in good manners, or presented by noble institutions, contain a deeper power.

This is not to say, for a minute, that the outright racial slur does not have a terrible force. I have Aboriginal comrades who have been injured, sometimes deeply, by explicit racism. A Noongar dude I know was asked by staff to strip his own bed after a night in a South Australian motel to save the white housekeeper from unnecessary contact with his "black germs." That such brutal ugliness can ever be thought is shameful. That it can be heard is almost unthinkable.

But the mass, unconscious ideology that otherwise shaped this Noongar man's life was far more brutal. He was stolen from his mother by a *caring* government with the *best* intentions. It's so much harder to fight the very naturalized, often very rational-sounding ideas about Aboriginal people held by white policy-makers than the crazed talk of a country motel manager. Yes, the declarations of that turd are to be condemned — and they were, by the Noongar man who countered with, "No need to change the sheets. I wore a hazmat suit to bed, because we all know your dive is as clean as a Coachella toilet." But, those politely expressed false sympathies of the political class — poor Aboriginal people can't handle their grog, poor Aboriginal people are welfare dependent, poor Aboriginal people aren't helping their case by being so angry — can't so easily be met with a Noongar zinger.

Which is to say, the undressed ideology of racist slurs is awful, but the concealed ideology, which still permits the theft of Aboriginal children and land, commits a polite violence on a monumental scale. In recent years, many Aboriginal people in Northern Territory communities were subjected, by government policy, to joining a particular queue at the supermarket. Their incomes were controlled "for their own good" and spending cards they were issued with only worked at a particular machine. The effect of all this was a daily experience of segregation. The "compassionate" government ideology delivers a message about your "black germs" every time you go to buy milk. I'm sure I don't need to explain why this ideology, expressed as policy, is far more of an outrage than the naked hatred from a single motel manager.

You can and must fix your own racism, transphobia, et cetera. You must *not* suppose that this individually noble act will be magically upscaled. It *does not* all start with you. It's not "all connected" in the easy way some might suppose. To believe that your personal purity and great compassion serves anyone so well as you is mystification.

Professor of Aboriginal History Gary Foley makes the case that Prime Minister Kevin Rudd's 2008 apology to the Stolen Generation was ideological. To the *Melbourne Historical Journal*, this scholar said that the show stitched up Aboriginal history into the service of the dominant white ideology. Rudd did not offer compensation to Aboriginal people of any kind, or any meaningful material plan to repair their awful circumstances for which successive Australian governments can be held responsible. He made no reference whatsoever to the Intervention in the Northern Territory, which at the time of writing quietly continues, now in its tenth year of brutal control over the lives of Aboriginal citizens. But, hey, Kevin said sorry. As far as Foley, whom I and many others consider a formidable thinker, was concerned, the "event will be a part of future white Australian mythology about how wonderfully they have always treated the Aboriginal people."

Clearly, the blubbering Rudd felt that he was doing something marvelous. Even as he cried real tears, the real lives of people in the

Territory were subject to legal intimidation, surveillance, and tight control over income spending and even, bizarrely, internet use. And all of this was based on the lie — it was found to be baseless — that Aboriginal men were enthusiastic pedophiles. This particularly vicious falsehood was first aired in the media not by the hard Right. It wasn't Andrew Bolt first calling "these people" rapists. It was lovely, liberal Tony Jones on the anti-racist ABC (Australian Broadcasting Corporation).

Bolt, an artless polemicist, is unabashed in his motel manager–style loathing. Many, many people who consider themselves "left wing" attack him openly. But the true obscenity, surely, is not his. Bolt did not cry while he wrote inflammatory garbage. Bolt has never been such a vulgar hypocrite that he'd pretend to give a shit about anything but his own class interests. Rudd and Jones, on the other hand, claim, through the powers of ideological mystification, to *care*.

Rudd and Jones mean well. I am certain they see themselves as actively opposed to racism. I am quite sure they would be shocked to see their actions described as being in the service of a racist, and capitalist, order. I am not entirely convinced, though, that we can say that these powerful men, so instrumental in the Intervention, were *completely* mystified. These guys must have had *half* a demystified clue.

Rudd knew what was going on in the Territory even as he cried for lost Aboriginal childhoods. The program of violence and control, which still permits police to enter private properties without a warrant, was authorized by him. Jones, surely, must have realized that he and the ABC played a role in bringing about the program that was later to be renamed, softly and ideologically, "Stronger Futures."

In 2012, the now-defunct Aboriginal affairs publication *Tracker* showed that *Lateline* focused on stories of child sexual abuse in Territory communities. *Lateline*'s own web archive records the broadcast of eleven stories of sexual abuse in the Territory in eight days. These included a particularly sensational report headlined "Sexual Slavery," which claimed that in the community of Mutitjulu, children were being held against their will then passed around Aboriginal men who would pacify them with rags soaked in gasoline. Huge if true, right? But the story turned out to be untrue.

The chief witness, shot in shadows to protect his identity and described as a Mutitjulu youth worker, turned out to be public servant Gregory Andrews, an assistant secretary in the Office of Indigenous Policy Coordination. A guy whose work it was to "coordinate" Aboriginal citizens, with a high level of influence, was portrayed only as a humble social worker, brought to tears by sexual abuse that the Territory police and the Australian Crime Commission later said lacked any credible evidence.

But the morning after the story went to air, before Andrews's allegations could be investigated and subsequently dismissed by these two agencies, a report was commissioned that would be called "Little Children Are Sacred." The report was widely praised. It recommended consultation with Aboriginal people and did not make allegations of widespread, organized pedophilia. But instead, it became the pretext for the Intervention begun by Prime Minister John Howard and continued under Rudd.

Chris Graham of *Tracker* was watching Tony Jones hosting *Q&A* on TV in 2012 as the Intervention was discussed. On the show, Aboriginal leader Rosalie Kunoth-Monks said that the chief work of the Intervention had been to "hunt us like dogs" — by many accounts, including those of Amnesty and many Christian

churches, a fair assessment. Jones asked the conservative polit-
ician Dave Tollner to respond. As Tollner's naked ideology came
up against Jones's more politely dressed form, there was a moment
of demystification. *Tracker* recorded the exchange:

> "Let's put some things into context here Tony, and I
> do acknowledge your role in the intervention ..." said
> Tollner.
>
> A clearly pissed off Jones interrupted. "I had no role
> in the intervention; that was done by a government."
>
> "No, no, no, but it was your show that lifted the lid
> on many of the problems that occur in remote com-
> munities and I acknowledge that," replied Tollner.
> "That led to the major inquiry that resulted in the
> Little Children Are Sacred report, so I do acknow-
> ledge your interest in this area."

Tollner is not the kind of guy I'd like to have over for scones.
But, his vulgar manner did demystify the act of which Jones had
been a part. Tollner is the kind of white guy that Martin Luther
King Jr. would have preferred, here. Better the outrageous conservative than the white moderate who paternalistically believes he
can set the timetable for another man's freedom.

Jones's claim that the Intervention was solely due to the government and that his program had no role was some *elaborate* mystification. Here, we have another case of what Marx describes as the
interweaving of the material with the idea.

There have been times where I have been ideological. I'm not
claiming to be a class-conscious angel. I have had shitty mystified
thoughts. These have included, "She only got that job because she's

a Millennial," and — I can't believe I'm telling you this — "Nobody would think that guy was such an interesting writer if he were not brown." These thoughts serve ageism and racism, but they chiefly served my faith in capitalism.

In both cases, I was lamenting my own lack of income and, like some kind of toilet Trumpist, I reached for an identity group to blame. To be honest, she *was* a good writer, and he was, and is, a *fantastic* one. I corrected these thoughts immediately and would never permit them to be uttered as fact — I'm only telling you about them now to make the case that I don't suppose for a minute that I'm purer than Tony Jones. In fact, I'm worse, as I've thought about how ideology takes hold in me for years, and I'm betting that Tony only thinks of ideology as something other people suffer. Also, I wasn't even trying to save entirely fictional children from made-up sexual abuse allegations. I was just being a brutal ideological asshole silently to myself.

For an instant, I served the master's ideas. "The ideas of the ruling class are in every epoch the ruling ideas," says Marx. Read that again. It's awesome. So is this: "The class which is the ruling material force of society, is at the same time its ruling intellectual force."

The hope for the Marxist is that they will be able to identify and so divest themselves of these ruling-class ideas. *This* Marxist has no hope that she will ever be able to convince Kevin and Tony that their actions were ideological, and served both racism and capitalism (as we've discussed, the idea of a hopeless class of people, such as in the racist USA, is very handy for maintaining concentrated material wealth). But I do know that in certain cases we can expose the way in which ideology is either cynically or naively used by the ruling class.

The strategy of cynically concealing one's power isn't exactly new. You have likely heard of Machiavelli, whose sixteenth-century treatise on effective dominance, *The Prince*, is still read by diplomats and businesspeople today. Old Mack is bang into the effective strategy of seeming nice. "A prince ought to take care that he never lets anything slip from his lips that is not replete with the ... qualities, that he may appear to everyone who sees and hears him as a paragon of mercy, loyalty, humanity, integrity, and scrupulousness." In other words, never try to win by force what can be gained by the appearance of kindness. Of course, if the appearance of kindness doesn't work, set your armed men on the fuckers.

What *The Prince* offered was not so much ideology as a handbook for realist cynics. So, it's not for the crying Kevin Rudd. Rudd is unlikely to make the admission, even to himself, that he was in the business of deluding the people; of knowingly having a sook about Aboriginal pain but actually causing Aboriginal pain. I'm sure he was far more genuine in his confusion than Machiavelli. Ideology and its applications change over time.

This is where one of Marx's ideas shows its age. Ideology is, as I have said, a strong and useful concept, but it is not a *method* of thinking, unlike historical materialism, that can survive the years intact. It's more of a description of a *thing* than a method of thinking, and later Marxists can be very valuable in expanding or updating that description. Before I describe the problem with the purely Marxist idea of ideology and offer solutions, here are some other Marxists' takes: Antonio Gramsci's idea of cultural hegemony is marvelous, and you can read that in his *Prison Notebooks*. György Lukács is beloved by many Marxists for his *History and Class Consciousness*, which is an excellent self-help guide for the working class that wants to get woke. Personally, I think Louis Althusser, in *Ideology and Ideological State Apparatuses*, goes on with a lot of French crap, but this could be due to my own stupidity. Although he is shunned by classical Marxists, for me Slavoj Žižek makes invaluable and entertaining updates to the concept of ideology. You can read his book, *The Sublime Object of Ideology*, or watch his bonkers film, "The Pervert's Guide to Ideology," on YouTube.

Žižek makes the case that ideology has become more complex and self-deluded since the nineteenth century. For Marx and Engels, ideology was a thing often deliberately prepared to mystify the working class. When those two guys met in a bar as young men to write *The German Ideology*, literacy rates were lower and mass media were not yet in existence. So, powerful people *could* circulate documents that described the maintenance of power among themselves with high confidence that Julian Assange wouldn't leak them.

*The Prince* predates the liberal era that Marx criticizes so well. You're not going to get advice to leaders like, "Pretend you're nice before you fuck them up," from Kant, Locke, or that jerk Voltaire. These Enlightenment guys on whom we base our current Western capitalist morals spoke a little more euphemistically about rights and reason, a bit more Jefferson style, with all that "Equality for everyone ... by which I mean guys like me!" stuff. These thinkers had become more ideological themselves and had also learned to mystify their blueprints for domination for the rising bourgeois class.

Nonetheless, you get some more blunt statements than you would from the powerful today. Check out this dazzler: "Civil government, so far as it is instituted for the security of property, is, in reality, instituted for the defence of the rich against the poor." This comes to us from the granddaddy of capitalism, Adam Smith. His work, *The Wealth of Nations*, was influential, and one which Marx was particularly eager to debunk. He charged Smith with great intellectual naivete, but he could not accuse Smith of mystifying his underlying assumptions. Which were that we need a government, and unfortunately must pay them a little tax, so that they can buy the stuff to defend us against the poor.

The ideas contained in *The Wealth of Nations*, from which the neoliberal economic policies we have today are essentially indistinct, became, and remain, the ideas of the ruling class. Although, it should be said that Smith — a guy who wrote so long ago — proposed a more progressive system of taxation of the rich than we see today.

As Engels wrote on ideology in a letter to a comrade in 1893, "It is above all this appearance of an independent history of state constitutions, of systems of law, of ideological conceptions in every separate domain, which dazzles most people." This "false consciousness" among the working poor was of an equal democracy that promised opportunity to the people. The ruling class knew, per Smith, that the state and the capitalists were in league to defend their riches. The working class were encouraged not to know this, and to believe the dazzling lie of the independent modern state. You know, that modern state built, in great part, by the ideas of Adam Smith.

If we want to understand the way a man of the present like Rudd thinks, Marx and Engels aren't quite so useful to us as Žižek. Žižek sees a new duality in the way ideology operates for the policy and ruling classes. In short, they have become a lot more convinced by their own bullshit. And we, the working class, have become less convinced by it.

Žižek formulates the structure of a classical Marxist ideology this way: "They do not know it, but they are doing it." In some cases, this can still hold true. My working-class relatives, for example, still believe that you can make it in Australia if you try, and do not, I suspect, believe that my failure to own a residence has much to do with prevailing economic conditions. To them, I am simply a lazy fucker. Their agemates in the press certainly have this opinion about Millennials. However, the Millennial working class, whom we so often accuse of achieving nothing but Tinder brunch dates, have begun educating themselves on house commodity prices. They have quit blaming themselves and, in some encouraging cases, have come to blame specific policies (remember, a Marxist *doesn't blame people).* There are many Millennials of my professional and personal acquaintance who will spout sentences like, "Of course, when the Treasurer applied the capital gains tax concession in 1999, this widened the gap between the investor and non-investor class already made possible by the longstanding state attachment to negative gearing." This is class consciousness, you guys, and it makes me so happy to see your ideology wither.

But what I see in our ruling classes is some ideological shuffling. When they write their shit about how young people aren't buying homes because they're too busy stuffing themselves with brunch and Tinder cock, there are two things going on. There is some of the, "They do not know it, but they are doing it," once the province of the working class, and also a dose of, as Žižek puts it, "They know it, but they are doing it anyway."

They are naive *and* cynical in their ideology at once. The ruling class don't know it *and* they do know it. *And*, they are still doing it.

If you dare, you can think of the Obama administration in this way.

Has there ever been another president who spoke so well and with such genuine compassion? Has there ever been a liberal nation with such a militarized police force, such widespread surveillance, such harsh penalties for whistleblowers, and such restrictions on press freedom?

We think Donald Trump is mean to the press and, *sure*, he openly derides them. But the gentler Obama *really* curtailed the ability of the press to do its job. In 2016, the Associated Press reported that President Obama's administration had "set a record for the number of times its federal employees told disappointed citizens, journalists, and others that despite searching they couldn't find a single page requested under the Freedom of Information Act."

Barack Obama may have adopted a kinder language to describe those who resided in the United States unofficially — calling them "undocumented" instead of "illegal" — but he also deported more of them than any previous president. Estimates of those deported range between 2.5 and 3 million people, and the *Independent* newspaper made the case that Obama "removed more undocumented migrants than the total sum of presidents in the twentieth century." Still, he was super nice about it, and while he was quietly perfecting the efficient deportation infrastructure that Donald Trump would later openly use, we were all so glad that here, finally, was a truly compassionate president. One who finished off his final year by dropping 26,171 bombs, and maintaining a military presence in 138 countries, "a staggering jump of 130 percent since the days of the Bush administration," observed the *Guardian*, in one of its less popular pieces. Liberal ideologues do not enjoy reading negative things about Obama.

Obama went in for a big compassionate finish, too. In his last days in office, he authorized the deployment of 4,000 US troops to the Russian border, largely based on the suspicion of a few intelligence community personnel that Russia had "hacked" the 2016 election. Russia did this, allegedly, by offering WikiLeaks documents and emails held by Hillary Clinton's campaign staff.

If you read these "Podesta" files, you'll find, inter alia, that President Obama accepted a Citigroup executive's advice on appointments to his cabinet. You'll find that Hillary Clinton told a group of immensely wealthy Goldman Sachs executives, in a speech for which she received a six-figure sum, that there were certain stories she would tell them, the elite, confidentially, and others she would tell the American people, who simply didn't understand confusing things like massive wealth accumulation.

If you can ever be bothered, read some of these Podesta emails. They are, at once, both cynical and naive. The document Citigroup sent for Obama's perusal is kind of amazing. It is clearly offering up a list of names that will act in the interests of that firm, but it does so very nicely. It even includes a list of choices for the president to make and has handy symbols so that he can see which appointments qualify as "diverse." So even though Michael Froman and Obama, who later appointed him as a US trade representative, were engaged in a financial conspiracy that makes what Martha Stewart did look like borrowing an envelope from the office stationery room, they were clearly very committed to equality for all ethnicities. At least, committed to equality for all ethnicities with nice jobs on Wall Street.

I mean COME ON. This is shocking, right? Obama took the suggestions of a money man whom he would later award a cushy, influential government post. This revelation was barely mentioned in the press, who had now begun to think of anything that might damage Clinton's election chances as unethical. They knew what they were doing, but they also didn't know. They lost sight of what truly occurred, which was, in any assessment, evidence that the White House was not doing anything but defending the rich against the poor.

No one in the Democratic Party has ever claimed that these documents were not genuine. As far as they were concerned, the real crime here, which would be avenged by moving tanks into Polish towns, was that someone, possibly not even the Russians, had told the truth. It wasn't that the president and his appointed successor were shown to be directly serving the interests of the finance sector. Who cares about that stuff, because, hell, Obama is so nice, and Clinton is an inspiring role model for our daughters. And they both defend the rich against the poor.

Again. This is NOT to make a case for Donald Trump, who is a broken toilet. Rather, it is to explain the mechanism of ideology.

Sometimes, we sniff out ideology when we are subject to its power, and it can present itself to us only as a feeling. I am really no fan of liberal feminism, but there is true value in the way that one of its most formative modern thinkers describes "the problem that has no name."

In the 1960s, Betty Friedan and others eventually gave that problem a name, and "sexism" became something we could identify. That Friedan initially characterized sexism as a malaise mysteriously contracted by women of the white middle class helps us understand the process of what Marx and other Marxists mean by "ideology." It is buried inside us. It can be as present in the people it diminishes as it is in those it benefits. It is upheld by the conditions of our labor — which, for this group of women, was often unpaid and largely domestic — and it can be reinforced by the state, as it can be by apparently inoffensive gestures, such as a man who tries to soothe an upset woman by patting her bum. (Pro tip: NEVER DO THIS, UNLESS ASKED.)

Oh, shit. Now I've gone and mentioned *feminism*, which has had such a long and troubled relationship with Marx. This is such a famously on-again off-again pair, they will receive an entire chapter of couples counselling to themselves. But let me say for now: gender relations *cannot* be comprehensively explained by Marx. Marx can't repair everything that is rotten in the world, and he never claimed that he could. But the liberal feminist description of sexist ideology, with which you are likely to be familiar, helps us understand the form of capitalist ideology, which you may not have thought about very much before.

Sexist ideology is always easier to see as its expressions age. We can look at old women's magazines that describe how to time a slow-cook casserole so that you have a spare hour to pop on a girdle and do your hair for hubby. People used to read this and find it unsurprising. This, we would have said back then, was just the natural way of things. It was women behaving as they might in a state of nature, which, as reliable paleontologists report, involved a lot of fussing with hot-rollers fashioned from the bones of Stone-Age cucks who had been eaten by ancient beasts.

It took a forthright liberal like Betty Friedan to point this out as hogwash. But, boy, did people give her a hard time. Just as people will give you a hard time today if you insist that a lot of women's media continues to be fixated on devouring women's time in the service of high-cost individuality.

Gwyneth Paltrow's newsletter, GOOP — which happened to launch the very month the Global Financial Crisis was officially declared — deluded women into feeling "empowered" by spending lots of money on exotic smoothies. Gwyneth compels her gender to increase their crippling personal debt and spend their time doing sex-slave bullshit so abject it makes a hot-roller look like a violent act of feminist revolution.

Gwyneth tells us gals to pop something called "Moon Juice Sex Dust" into our organic kale juice. Give the GOOP store thirty

US dollars, and receive, "a lusty edible formula alchemized to ig-nite and excite sexy energy in and out of the bedroom." Gwyneth has written in praise of the expensive vaginal steam clean — pre-sumably, an act of hygiene urgently required after a heavy dose of Sex Dust. Anyhow. *You* try telling a liberal feminist that Gwynnie is a douche-selling douche. They will, quite perversely, tell you that you are being sexist and undermining a strong woman's success. They'll keep saying that until this era's respected Betty Friedan reveals to us all that Gwyneth has been quietly working for our misogynist capitalist overlords. I mean, I tried to tell my sisters, but they all think I'm a "brocialist" and therefore not to be trusted.

I'll wait, though. Ideology reveals itself over time. I would pre-fer it revealed itself instantly. But, in the Gwyneth case, at least I know I got in early and will one day be able to claim, like Marx, that "I told you so."

On the matter of the ideological defence of capitalism, Marx told us so more than 150 years ago. Across his many works, he engages with the economic thinkers of the Enlightenment age and powerfully illustrates their rich GOOP-level shit.

Ideology is not always visible to us. The Marxist holds that the least visible kinds of power are also the most effective. Accordingly, the Marxist, in my view, must defy these power structures by mak-ing her own beliefs as plain to herself as she will to others. The Marxist must get into the habit of seeing *and* telling the truth about capitalism.

There *are* Marxists who try to persuade others of the power their doctrine by what they think are subtle means — if you've ever been to an LGBTI protest, you'll find a Trotskyist there saying, "Same-sex marriage is wonderful, isn't it? I just love the written approval of the state! Let me read you some relevant literature." I do not go in for any of that and, really, if we're honest, Marx didn't either.

In the last paragraph of *The Communist Manifesto*, Marx is unambiguous about the need for communists to be frank.

> The Communists disdain to conceal their views and aims. They openly declare that their ends can be attained only by the forcible overthrow of all existing social conditions. Let the ruling classes tremble at a Communistic revolution.

Pretty clear on the honesty front, if you ask me. Find the capitalist ideology within yourself so you can openly declare your forcible overthrow of it to others.

Telling the "truth" from within capitalism isn't easy, even to yourself. It's certainly no fun. It must, however, have an upside. Please let me know when you find it.

# 4

## "OMG"! You Are Totally Extracting Profit From My Body And My Mind! And I Only Just Met You On The "Tinder Book"!

f you've skipped the chapter on ideology and think that you're ready for one on labor, bend over for a slap. *There.* Bad Marxist! Who told you this whole transforming-the-mode-of-production thing was going to be cookies and cream? Harden the fuck up, comrade. Go back and eat your wholemeal pain-cake. I can wait all night.

Okay, I'm sorry. You don't *have* to turn back those pages. Your time, after all, is money. As a member of the so-called "gig econ-omy," which is French for "bad credit," I know this very well. Let me make it quicker for you, before we both return to the problem of our everyday survival.

Almost everything you need to know right now about the mys-tifying effect of ideology on work can be experienced in today's job interview.

You face the recruitment panel, these strangers with the power to decide your fate. Perhaps, like Comrade Razer, you have a taste for the dramatic, and you imagine this as a form of deep state torture. Especially when they say, Tell Us About Your Greatest Weakness.

If you want to join the fascists, you say, "My true weakness is that sometimes I work too hard and need to be reminded to stop." If you want to die on a gulag, you say, "My true weakness is the need to binge-watch awful fantasy programming on Netflix as I use a tube of Pringles to fill the emptiness inside me. On these sad days, I will text you at five minutes past nine and say that I have acid reflux. Expect this to happen at least once a month."

You don't tell the truth. You say that you're a perfectionist. That you demand too much of yourself, just like those amazing people we see in Aaron Sorkin dramas. That the *only problem* any boss has ever previously detected in you is your unwillingness to sleep in your own bed instead of the office, because work is where you most love to be, President Jeb!

You know this is a mystification. They know this is a mystifica-tion. But, you both know that this, or some version of it, needs to be said.

What we all know you are truly saying in this moment is, "I understand that I will give more value to the company than the company will offer to me." You are cautiously admitting the thing Marx was once able to make dangerously clear to millions: the capitalist is the only one who profits from the bodies and minds of the workers.

This relationship between you and your employer may seem almost too obvious to utter, but let's say it again anyway: you give your employer greater value than they give you. This is not an equal relationship. Your labor *must* bring more profit to the company than you are paid.

When you return home from work, you leave behind the goods or services you have produced. You retain no right to them. If you take what you have produced, you have broken the law. If you borrow some of the tools used for this production, you have broken the law. Even if you helped make that damn tool, whether a piece of software or a fix for a robot arm or a set of occupational safety protocols or sexual harassment guidelines that could benefit others, it remains the property of the capitalist employer, and to take back this useful thing you made is to break the law.

So, when we make the ideological hint, as most of us must in these job interviews, that we are the sort who will work just a little harder than those other lazy, thieving candidates, we are agreeing to these rules of capitalist labor. Many of us rationalize this agreement to ourselves by means of a *West Wing* fantasy in which the truly great society is built and won by individuals who are super good at their jobs. We then agree to the false idea that merit decides who wins. We agree to the unethical idea that those who have more merit should have more property. We agree to imagine ourselves as ultracompetent powerbrokers walking through unending corridors as we utter our unending wisdom.

We begin to make another agreement. This is to what Marx called our "alienation" — which sounds even more marvelously depressing, as most things do, in the original German, *Entfremdung*.

Even as everyday people in the West have largely forgotten Marx's whole deal with the capitalism-is-intrinsically-evil thing, they tend to hold with this part of his work. You may, as I do, use the word *alienation* from time to time in everyday speech. You may use it to describe that sense of feeling alone while surrounded by others, of weird confusion in the supermarket. You have Marx largely to thank for popularizing this concept and word.

It may appear to you that the idea of alienation just *is*; that we'd have it with or without Dr. Marx. Of course, we would have come up with another way to account for and describe that common sensation of distance. So many of us feel removed from things to which we know we should feel very close. But, without Marx and his idea of alienation, we would not have had many of the great works of cinema and literature and song that form our view of it today. This is a good thing to remember in general: whether we know it or not, our minds hold onto philosophical concepts written down long ago. These can be useful ones, like Freud's unconscious or Marx's alienation, or they can be really shitty ones, like the "natural law" of capitalism, proposed by every capitalist bastard from the time of John Locke.

Anyway. Enough of reminding you *again* that your ideas always have a history — a *material* history. And enough, for the present, with the idea that work as we know it is "natural" — we'll examine the view that capitalist labor is organized by some sort of sexy, competitive biological drive later on. Let's stick for now with the idea of our alienation.

The Young Marx describes four kinds of alienation. As this is not a textbook and you are very busy, let's forget about a full examination of each and just list them quite briefly, leaving the committed revolutionary to read the *Economic and Philosophical Manuscripts of 1844* one day when she is off work, eating chips, and pretending to have gastro. (I generally encourage all workers to do this.)

You are, first, alienated from the product of your labor. It's not yours. You don't get to keep it. You are, second, alienated by the method of production. You usually only get to make a little part of it. This is as true for the corporate paralegal working on a series of intellectual property clauses as it is for the people who once worked in the car factories of Detroit. Third, you are alienated from what Marx sees as your "essence" as a producer — we humans like to make and do and plan. This attribute, he says many years later in *Capital*, is what "distinguishes the worst architect from the best of bees ... the architect raises his structure in imagination before he erects it in reality." Fourth, you are alienated from your fellow producers. You are divided from them, sometimes physically, and you *must* see them as competition. This division of labor can often occur along cultural lines, too. We get women's work and brown people's work and by these means, we get more cultural division.

When we talk about alienation in the present West, we talk about it in the same way we talk about a lot of other problems: as if we are living on a dream Apple cloud where we have all overcome our physical needs. We see ourselves as creatures who are affected *only* by the way we *think* about things. We negate the material, a way of modern Western thinking that some Marxists like to call "post-material."

Let's look at an example of large-scale post-materialism. Since 2012, the United Nations has published something called a World

Happiness Report to compare the fortunes of nations. This liberal organization decided that "well-being" and "happiness" were to be the new indicators of a life well lived. The report was initially subtitled "A new economic paradigm," because, apparently, those other measurements — sanitation, purchasing power, freedom from hunger and airstrikes — were just so old hat.

The new preference of the United Nations to measure the immeasurable can also be seen in the 2016 Sustainable Development Goals, a new set of objectives that look like something I might have addressed to Dear Diary when I was thirteen. It's all "inclusion" and "save the planet" with the merest possible reference to those production and consumption practices that exclude so many people and trash the planet. As life on Earth becomes a problem, our institutional solution appears to be to pretend it occurs elsewhere.

We can say that a lack of clean water doesn't matter so much in the Global South when we have a UN document to say that its people are "happy." We say that the real cause of poverty is people thinking racist thoughts, but do not stop to see military force and trade sanctions applied to countries that are entirely populated by brown people. Is an act of UN awareness-raising *really* going to turn US foreign policy around? The post-materialist thinks so. The historical materialist does not.

We also say, in the case of our alienated feelings, that these are simply the result of people just not caring anymore and being too busy with their iPhones, et cetera. I think, for all the shortcomings that history imposes on Marx's description of the way we work, that we must again tie the idea of our alienation to our labor.

The way we gain the means for our survival comes to inform the way that we think. The way we spend most of our waking life changes us. What we do all day, for money or to pass the time, marks us. It marks many of the policymakers at the United Nations — the World Happiness Report strikes me as a document monumentally alienated from the hungry world it seeks to describe.

We can easily see the way some groups of people are influenced by the way they spend their time. We don't, largely, have any trouble with tying the alienation of, say, 4chan users, to the way they spend their physical lives. When people on the /b/ board started to support, however ironically, the idiocy of Donald Trump, there were a thousand articles and a million memes (memes, incidentally, were first the product of 4chan's unpaid labor, so the next time you say something mean about 4chan, remember they gave us internet cats) explaining *why* these guys were *like* this — which is to say, so alienated from the idea of the common good. They live in their parents' basements, people said; 4chan users themselves joke about this openly. This largely male, self-identified heterosexual group have never felt the touch of a woman, was another rationale. Again, the men of 4chan will admit to this, and "ironically" celebrate disembodied robot vaginas. They are isolated. They have, we say, no hope in their lives. And it's hard to argue with that when you see the product of their collective labor. Those lulz aren't so full of kittens anymore.

The true Marxist will say that their hope has evaporated largely due to the conditions of the market, while the liberal will say, along with the right-wing conservative — from whom they have become, in economic matters, indistinct — that these guys just weren't trying hard enough to make it. They're sexless toxic white men who resent the disappearance of their privilege et cetera.

Whatever your view of 4chan and those other keyboard warriors of the alt-right — and let's be clear for those up the back, I am profoundly opposed to racism, ableism, transphobia, et cetera — you can probably see that the conditions of their lives produce a certain kind of alienation, for which they compensate by coming together online to call each other "beta cucks" and perform acts of mock-rape in World of Warcraft, or whatever. You can see that their material experience — which in this case is largely virtual and physically smells of old cheese — plays a great role in their alienation.

Well, samesies for you, as Marx said in his Address of the Central Committee to the Communist League. *No, he didn't. JK. Lol. Do you think I'm serious, cuck? Become An Hero.* That's the entire sum of my 4chan literacy, and you can expect no more.

As I mentioned in that previous chapter you so stubbornly refused to read, even a fully conscious awesome Marxist comrade like Helen can feel alienated from her fellow workers. When you're working for the very least the capitalist can get away with paying you — and this is *always* the case; if it were not, capitalists would not make a profit and would no longer be capitalists — you are, in fact, in competition with others. If these others are more profitable to the capitalist than you, you know that you are under threat. Some people argue that this fear "drives productivity," and I'm sure in many cases it does. But, this is where we must admit that we may, like Marx, be moral people and ask ourselves: is the emotional (and material) poverty of that life worth the prize of profit?

If the majority of the world's population, whether they be 4chan trolls or Chinese factory workers, are just feeling lost, what's the point? If the way we spend our working days is in the production of personal turmoil, or the way we spend our enforced leisure is in the creation of social turmoil in the form of racist memes, then *what* the actual fuck? Setting aside the mass decline in real Western wages, the enslavement of entire nations and that whole one billion starving people thing, an end to our sad and deep estrangement is surely something even the liberal must consider.

If they can't make it to their factory dormitories, some workers in the Global South fall asleep at the workstations that produce the commodities upon which the boys of /b/ will create macro atrocity. These guys may even make a meme depicting a suicidal Chinese worker. You know, just for lulz.

You can be all very, "But that's just a few people, most of us are happy," if you like. This is an elite form of alienation. Because you do know, beneath that mystification, that this is not the case for most — we don't just shrug and accept the fact of one billion starving people who could be fed with the wealth of eight dudes, and we don't just meet very widespread racism with, "You guys need to think better thoughts." You also know that at one point or another, your own work has produced in you a sense of alienation. You have felt estranged. You have thought, "What's the point?" You've been tempted to chuck it all in, or you have begun to resent the hell out of the person working next to you for no identifiable reason at all. If this is not the case, then you have been very fortunate. As I've said — and I truly mean this — if your life is good, I'm happy for you. I want what you have for everyone.

You can put the sad state of the human world down to individual greed, if you wish. You can blame that bad person or that bad human tendency for the sense of isolation you may have felt at work, or in relation to your government-provided income — the recipient of social security income knows the paralysis of alienation better than most. Or, you could say, as Marx does, albeit in a very scientific way toward the end of his writing life, that what we need is to build *hope* for ourselves into the mode of production.

---

We don't do this by hashtagging #hope and waiting for it to arrive. We need to build it into our mode of production.

Let's say that some people are greedy and will always be greedy and were just born that way. This may well be true in an individual sense — I, for example, forget all my communist principles when it comes to sharing meringues — but scaling that up still doesn't result in a world in which eight men now command more wealth than the poorest half of it. The present imbalance, which makes feudal power as evenly distributed among humans as acne, did not come about due to a lack of human virtue alone.

Capitalist enterprise, as you might have heard successful idiots say, demands a "Kill or be killed" approach. Which is to say, to succeed in business, you must squeeze the most out of everyone for the least. I mean, *shit*. Even to "succeed" as a *shopper*, you must do this. This T-shirt (I'm still wearing it, and, man, it does *not* smell good) cost three dollars. How in the name of Hayek does a T-shirt cost three dollars, and why is it the only one that I can comfortably afford? Who got hurt? Can I put it all down to human greed, or do I get to say that it is the capitalist mode of production that largely produced this pain? Can I finally see the *material* in this T-shirt?

It's not just cruel textile barons and blithe Western journalists who create this pain. We are all compelled to participate in it. Even woke workers must be assholes. Even rainforest-safe coffee consumers pay for exploitation. Even nice capitalists must engage in "greedy" practices.

Let's say that you're a very nice person who runs a vegan café. You use no animal products. You play only independently produced music, furnish only with upcycled objects. Still, the "free market" demands that you behave in a dominating way that may feel very unnatural to you.

To be very vulgar about it, you must fuck with people for your business to survive, let alone flourish. First, your employees must provide you with labor whose value to you is greater than the wages you provide them — you take from them what Marx calls a "surplus." You use these persons as instruments of profit. On your balance sheets, they appear as commodities you must buy. Then, your customers must pay more for your chocolate avocado pudding than it cost you in labor and goods to make. You are forced to do this by that "free" and "natural" market. You don't have any choice.

I am, of course, very pleased that the rights of no beasts were infringed in the production of your for-profit dessert. I applaud your efforts to showcase local art. I respect that you need to make a living and I am, within the terms of our current mode of production, very glad you can survive at this small scale. But you and I both know that to run at a profit, which is what one must do to stay in business, is to short-change others. You are marking these others as a "loss."

It's not that you, the vegan proprietor, are an immoral person. You don't lack virtue, and you feel very deeply for all creatures. But capitalism demands that you *lose* your virtue and become, in your every transaction, competitive. It's not, as your relatives may tell you, the other way 'round. Capitalist transactions make us competitive. Our competitive spirit did not make us capitalists. Still, people will tell you about "greed" being the problem, and the true root of all capitalist inequality.

Remember? "It is not the consciousness of men that determines their existence, but their social existence that determines their consciousness." This is one of those handy Marx travel wipes you should keep on your person for when a dirty capitalist comes near.

People fuck people under capitalist labor conditions, even if this is not their instinct or intention. We're all alienated. Think not just of the vegan café owner, but this time of the celebrated Bill Gates.

This guy, the world's second-wealthiest individual at the time of publication, is widely praised for his charitable works. Nice guy. Wants to cure malaria. If we look at his stewardship of Microsoft, where he built the foundation for his enormous fortune, we don't find too many stories about bad employer practices. What we have before us today is a guy whose personal net worth is roughly equivalent to the GDP of Slovakia. Bill Gates is equivalent to a nation. But he didn't build his virtual nation-state through good vibes.

He built his fortune not through personal greatness or even professional virtue. Sure, the guy was a decent programmer, but his operating system is no better than Android or Linux or macOS. Even leaving aside the old Silicon Valley drama in which the young and ambitious Gates claimed the work of other programmers as his own, his is not a story of personal wickedness any more than it is of personal virtue. It's just a story of everyday capitalism, in which he happened to be the winner.

Gates dodged taxes where he legally could, appropriated the work of others where it was permitted, and formed business arrangements that effectively shut his competitors out, consigning many of us office workers to a lifetime of Windows. He also did quite a bit to push for patents law, which had the effect of putting pharmaceutical drugs beyond the reach of many sick Americans. He may have not meant from the outset to become so obscenely wealthy, so protective of his assets. But to preserve his initial business success, he did.

Why in the name of Marx's housekeeper — which was, by the way, Helene Dumuth — Gates now wants to keep building his wealth via his holding and investment company is anybody's guess. The guy probably thinks he has earned the right to rule the world, and feels he has been elected in dollars. Who knows what happens to people once they become more individually powerful than entire nations. They never tell us, and we can only guess that they spend their evenings masturbating to the image of Jed Bartlet. What we do know, however, is that an extraordinarily wealthy man whose partial ownership of auto, biotech, food, beverage, hotel, agricultural equipment, and waste management companies is going to result in a lot of exploitation. Even if he does cure malaria, he's still greedy. Capitalism, the thing that now delivers the money to his door without him lifting a finger, made him that way.

It may be true that some of us are naturally greedy — seriously, *never* permit me near your meringues (unless they are vegan meringues, in which case, I will probably pass). It is certainly true that we are all creatures of great self-interest, some of us less able to balance our own needs against those of our fellows. But what is not true, for a Marxist, is that capitalism is the large-scale expression of this individual greed. It isn't natural. It certainly isn't free. We *could* behave in a very different way. If only we were not so alienated from our natures, so very far from freedom.

I should say at this point that not all your feelings of anger, isolation, depression, anxiety, misery and distress can be traced back to the capitalist mode of production. There can be deeper illnesses that have their roots, we presume, in nature. I say "presume" not, for a minute, to discredit the serious depressive illnesses and mood disorders that many people face. I say it because, at this point in the history of medical science, this remains a presumption. There is no blood test or brain scan to diagnose serious depression. You're not

going to find evidence of anxiety in your urine. There is no biological marker for loneliness.

About the only problem of mental illness for which there is
emerging sound genetic evidence is anorexia nervosa — and,
strangely, this dreadful and paralyzing state is the single one for
which we actually *do* blame capitalism. We say that skinny high
fashion models are to blame, even if anorexia scholars and anorexia sufferers tell us differently. The rest, though? We say that it's all
in our "chemicals"; that depression is just something that happens.
This has several dreadful consequences.

First is that psychiatry has largely abandoned the old distinction between mental illness that arises with a cause and
mental illness that just happens for no traceable reason at all.
Hippocrates, the official Father of Modern Medicine, wrote about
depressive-type disorders in this way: melancholy with an ex-
ternal cause, and melancholy that seemed to come from within. This important distinction was lost, with so much else, in the
1990s. You may think this means nothing for you, or your depressed mates. But what it means is an end to the "innovation,"
in this case within psychiatric science, we keep hearing so much
about. The need to sell drugs that seemed to work on some people with depressive illness meant that all people with depressive
illness were categorized identically. Now, people with depressive
illness are treated and studied in the same way. There are many
eminent psychiatrists, including Dr. Allen Frances, a former
editor, now critic, of the influential Diagnostic and Statistical
Manual of Mental Disorders, who have been very clear that this
impedes both research and cure. If we don't start to make medical distinctions between the people who are depressed because
they have been beaten by life and those who are depressed for

no identifiable reason at all, we learn little about anything but symptoms. A doctor meets a deeply alienated worker. She sees that the patient presents exactly as one who has enjoyed a life of leisure. She offers identical cures. It's a bit like treating a dizzy spell without first asking the patient, "Did you just come off a roundabout?" and immediately diagnosing them with stroke. Thanks for the "innovation," capitalism.

A second consequence is that we have spread the myth that mental illness is an equal-opportunity deal. "It can happen to anyone!" say the awareness commercials. "Even a CEO!" Now, while this is true and we concede the high likelihood of some mental illness having nature as its basis, what this thinking, which turns into policy, achieves is more of that big old post-material fuckup. Rates of depressive disorders and suicide are much higher in populations beset by poverty and poor work conditions. There *has* to be a reason that Aboriginal citizens are twice as likely to die by suicide than non-Aboriginal citizens, that some Aboriginal communities have up to *six-hundred times* the national rate of suicide, that the US Center for Disease Control reported in 2015 that serious psychological distress occurred at a rate of 8.7 percent in poor families. This National Health Interview Survey found that families living on an income four times the poverty rate, around US$80,000 per annum, were four times less likely to suffer this distress than those below the poverty line, at US$20,000. That's some alarmingly neat arithmetic.

A third is that we forget that even when people suffer such extreme estrangement that they seek to kill themselves, not everything in life is just in our heads. Sometimes, surely, the material world puts it there. We do not live in a post-material world where happiness cleans the water.

Yes. Not *everything* bad in life can be attributed to the capitalist mode of production. But what we have before us now, comrades, are a bunch of people insisting that *none* of the bad and alienating feelings we hold within us can be.

We have been deluded into thinking that every rotten feeling or act in the world can be traced back only to rotten people, or rotten genes. I want to tell you how we lost what was once very widespread impatience with the conditions of our work, or of our joblessness, in a society that values Sorkin-level job success.

People like me took this from you. I am referring specifically to my fellow fuckwits of the media class. It's not just avowedly right-wing press that prompts us to forget about things like wages anymore; it's also liberal media.

Now, it's not that those of us who make a living as media providers are awfully well remunerated. I earn around $50,000 (US$29,500) gross a year, which is the national median, and typical for workers in my sector. My point being that my industry peers and I are not rubbing foie gras into our necks every night to preserve our youthful tone. We are reminded of the material every day by our modest and insecure wage.

However, we work with texts and images. So, we're quite an unusual group of workers in that we are not fully alienated from the product of our labor — this book commodity, for example, may be owned in large part by its publisher, but I retain, as I do when I write short articles for the press, a sense that it is mine. We are not alienated by the method of production — this book is the result of the labor of many, but I retain the sense that I wrote it. The author or journalist or broadcaster is not especially alienated from their "essence" of being a producer, as we all tend to feel, and often truly are, empowered in the act of creation. We do not have the explicit sense, as so many workers do, of being divided from our colleagues. This is, in part, because we have the great cultural privilege of our station; people tend to think we are important, and this blinds us to the reality that others are conscious they are thought of as unimportant. And even though we are paid, in general, very little for our work, we often have the delightful experience of working closely with a talented editor or a publisher. So, for us, it's like: *What* alienation? Why don't you feel rewarded in your work as I do! Work. It might not pay much, but, boy, it's meaningful. Like it is for CJ in *The West Wing*.

The other thing that protects us media types from the harsh emotional conditions of work is the means of our production. Our tools are easily seized by us. We can take our literacy home. We know that these tools are very important; after all, they are used to create meaning itself! We culture makers have always been, in part, post-material creatures, so it's really no surprise that we, the arrogant creators of popular ideas, got right on board with this whole post-material trip. The post-material world says that ideas are the only important thing. This means journalists consider themselves *very* important, perhaps the MOST important, next to maybe scientists and technocrats and Jed.

Journalists are currently in a state of shock, having recently learned that people who are not journalists consider them not just unimportant, but actual scum. Journalists reporting just how marginalized they felt at Trump rallies became routine. "They hate us," said the dispatches, as though this were a surprise. Of course people alienated in their employment or unemployment are going to despise a group like us who never feel alienation in its keenest form, and so rarely report on the conditions of the working poor.

Yes, I may earn about the same as a middle manager at Target, but I do not deal with one tenth of the brutal, alienating shit experienced in discount retail. And, no, it doesn't really matter that I'm a Strong Woman Who Gets Trolled Online. Sure, that stuff is awful. But, given that I am able to turn it off, then speak to wide audiences about the pain of it and be called courageous for both acts, it's not that bad. It's not nearly as bad as being forced by your boss to sack people, chase down destitute shoplifters, or interrogate the Sudanese guy who is suffering PTSD and has unwittingly lingered in the consumer electronics department for a period deemed by the plainclothes security officer to be "too long." Give me "You are too ugly to rape" on my Facebook page over that rot every time.

Journalists claim that they are telling the "truth," but this truth is so often about ideas. The *New York Times* is filled to its margins with the naive contributions of a Brooks or a Krugman or a Kristof asking, "Why are people so unkind?" The *Sydney Morning Herald* is crammed with post-material rot urging the need for more powerful women on TV. Because we all know that the emergence of a sassy television lady has immediate effects for the majority of women, who work in unrewarding part-time jobs. But for a lack of true diversity in the culture, we would all be free. Really? All I need is a few more inspiring role models and belief in myself, and someone will give me a flat in which I can eventually die without fear that the landlord will interrupt my final breath with a housing inspection?

Get fucked with your "truth" and your "post-truth." The only thing like "truth" in the liberal press of the present can be found in its financial pages, where we see statements about magnificent profit. The real loss occurs in the remainder of the publication, given over almost entirely to moral lectures on how people who do not read this publication are shit.

And, yes, people who read those other right-wing publications, often owned by Rupert Murdoch, have shit ideas. No, I do not wish to befriend them. As for the people whose work they consume? Well, I yearned to physically break the fingers of late bigot Bill Leak. But I don't do this, and not just because I, a soft knowledge worker, lack physical strength, but because I know it wouldn't do any damn good. (Okay, maybe a bit of good.) I know that the real fight is not with those powerful communicators on the Right, who are irredeemable scum, but with the cloud-dwelling, listicle-loving, post-material idealists who claim that they are "Lefties," but write with all the material insight of a poached vegan meringue.

If you do not address the workers, the workers will not listen. If all you do is talk to others in your knowledge class, then the only people who will buy your "We need to think better thoughts" air-wank will be those who work in advertising and graphic design. If you really think that corporate events managers and social media strategists are the vanguard for change, by all means, keep writing about the need to use respectful language on Twitter.

If you want to engage with the lives of most people, you might consider looking where they work. They work in retail. In construction. In health care. When your reader has just finished cleaning an elder whose own body and mind have been worn down by decades of alienating factory labor, do you think that you bring much to their experience as a carer in a low-cost aged care facility with your piece on how people just don't *get* the important things in life? Please enjoy this slideshow of the Seven Most Empowering Sitcoms and remember to always be nice.

If this is not "post-truth," then my man Karl was a guy who wrote fables about princes on dream clouds.

We are fighting against our own alienation. We are fighting for the lives of our comrades in the Global South. We are fighting for a communist future full of free time. One in which, when the collective interview panel of the future asks us, as we apply for our six-hour-per-week participation, to Tell Us About Your Greatest Weakness, we'll answer that we used to believe in capitalism.

# 5

## "Bro" Marx Loves The Ladies! Or, As You Young Moderns Perhaps Know Them, "The Sister Powers!" LOL

I f this chapter on ladies is the first to which you have turned, you may be disappointed. Let's just get one thing straight, then: Marxism can't fix all sexism. Marxism is not the sort of thing that encourages anyone, not even ladies, to think special thoughts about their identity. Never said it was. These things are off the menu.

What Marxism proposes is that we the workers, of every identity, come together to take back the abundance built by us. In this moment of unity, the division of gender, or of any other identity, must not be our primary focus. We make this sacrifice — all of us — to do something enormous: transform the mode of production. What was held and managed privately becomes our collective stuff. Which, if you missed it, is *totally* okay, because we made all that stuff with our collective bodies and minds in the first place.

Look, we've been through this, but you femmos — so often troubled by the totalizing Marx — may need reminding. That change we will make to the world, enacted by our unquestioning unity, is one we *need* to make. Because, we want to both feed the hungry and thrill the interminably bored, right? Marxism means that the hungry and the bored will determine the shape of their interesting and well-fed futures together and need not wait for some generous Silicon Valley lass to think them worthy, to reward them for "leaning in" as per the capitalist yoga. Marx wants us all to be able to freely seize a good life every day. Not loiter till it's provided by another.

Marxism also means — you *cheeky* feminist, who skipped an entire first chapter on how material history produces dumb ideas — a pause in the production and distribution of big, very dumb ideas. Dumb ideas like, "Women are naturally drawn to purchase pastel-hued benchtops," and, "Chicks. They're not to be trusted with soldering irons, fishing rods, or the future of the world." The production of such ideas is only possible under capitalism. Marxism means an end to capitalism in favor of something better, and so the end to the production of such ideas. But, unfortunately, it *doesn't* mean an end to all forms of the thing we call sexism. Any Marxist who tells you that it does is a douchebag and quite possibly a liar.

Yes, some Marxists will tell that lie. They say it so unquestioningly that I have been moved to walk out of their meetings. They say that with the end of capitalism comes the total death of all unfavorable relations between women and men, which suggests to me that they are prepared to repeat history as farce. Are you *really* telling me that there was no sexism before capitalism, and that there shall be none after it? That rape — that act of violent control perpetrated every day — is entirely due to the mode of production? You say this, although Marx — who was quite aware of the division between the sexes — never made this claim himself. You're not supposed to use *Capital* to fill your commie bong and smoke all your worries away, comrade — you are *supposed* to read it.

Before we go on to (a) fully admit that a Marxist project will not solve all sexism and that feminism will long be needed, and (b) broadly predict the experience of being a lady or a non-lady on a post-capitalist planet — and *don't give me* that you can't indulge the fantasy of communist life, when I can say *for a fact* you've imagined being best friends with Solange, because I have, too, even knowing that the chances of a bloodless revolution by the workers are much higher than me attaining Ms. Knowles' private number — let us remember this whole worker thing one more crazy time. We are *all* workers. All of us outside of the one percent of the one percent, that is. Yes. Again. *Even* the people we don't personally like.

In a true resistance, the workers will stand together. Queer midlife blind Marxist women will stand shoulder to shoulder with dudes who voted for Trump. White dudes who voted for Trump will stand with brown women in hijabs, who will also stand with their Aboriginal comrades. We might not like it, but we will all agree to set aside our many cultural and identity divisions for long enough that we can topple that really big division that has not changed for so long: private ownership. We will stand together to achieve this. That's just how it works. It won't work any other way. You want to achieve a good material life for all the workers of the world while not actually feeling any shared bond with them? Soz. To employ the wisdom of the internet's most memed kittens, You Cannot Haz.

This doesn't mean the Marxist erases the fact of these identity divisions, or excuses acts of gender- or other identity-based aggression. The Marxist erases these identity divisions in favor of unity only during the struggle.

By contrast, what the liberal type of gal seeks to do is erase gender division for all time, but without addressing that whole "Does everyone in the world have enough to eat?" question we Marxists are so hungry to answer. Many of these liberal feminists don't really think that equality means anything more than the right to compete — you can even hear this in Beyoncé's song "Flawless," which she famously performed at the MTV Video Music Awards in front of that "feminist" sign, cut out as a backdrop standing fifteen feet tall. The song samples Nigerian author Chimamanda Ngozi Adichie, who says that she wants women to be free from the pressure to marry so that they may otherwise compete. Competition, says Adichie, "can be a good thing."

Liberal feminists are always going on about competition and the need to have women on boards. They don't have a problem with wealth inequality or private ownership. All they seek is the opportunity for all women, maybe all the people of the world, to have the equal right to secure their unequal share of wealth. They think society should be a case of rewarding "merit" and that if we just got rid of sexism, or other forms of cultural prejudice, the biggest rewards will naturally flow to the sassiest Sheryl Sandberg type. They believe that inequality is inevitable and that the capitalist mode of production, which has always left some people hungry, is just a reflection of nature. What they offer is an only slightly modified version of capitalism. It's "natural" to compete and profit from the labor of others, they say, while saying also that sexism is "unnatural." Dunno how they can claim one form of oppression to be natural and the other not. I suspect it is through decades of commitment to corporate success, which involves a great deal of *not* thinking.

Liberal feminism, the dominant kind of feminism at present, holds that inequality is fine. It's just that the inequality should be determined by natural merit, rather than by gender. (N.B. Whenever anybody says "meritocracy" in front of you in future, please scoff loudly.)

We have our liberal feminists. Then we have the ladies who are a little more sensitive to hardship. We might call these feminists Left-liberals. These people see poverty as a problem, but they see it as necessarily tied to sexism, racism, et cetera. While it is true that the poorest in the world are overwhelmingly the brownest and the lady-est, it is also true, in the Marxist view, that poverty under capitalism is inevitable. You simply cannot *have* capitalism without wealth inequality, says the Marxist (and anyone else who is honest about the nature of capitalism). If you do not agree to give up your body and mind for somebody else's profit, then capitalism ends. And even if we erase all the sexism and the racism through a series of awareness groups taught at all schools everywhere — even, apparently, places where the schools have been bombed to the shitter by the United States of America — what we still have is a capitalist mode of production. Which demands material inequality. Which demands an ideology. An ideology that says, "Those people have nothing because they didn't work hard enough." And frankly, if we begin to say this about any group — whether they are people with small noses, or people who are not obviously energetic, or people who are white and male — I don't really see how we're any better off. If you make the claim that racism or sexism causes poverty and you do not see that poverty is the first and biggest child of capitalism, you accept that capitalism *can* work fine and dandy. If only it were a little bit *nicer* to people.

There are even some feminists who claim that they are Marxist, notably UK writer Laurie Penny, who just think that the material Left needs to sort out all its problems with culture and identity *before* seizing the means of production. The most common criticism such Marxist feminists make of Marxism is that it is too *Marxist*. There is an open letter online you can read called "We Are The Left" whose signatories are nearly all feminists. These feminists say that the thing the Left *really* needs to do before it can seize the means of production is to call out its own sexism, racism, transphobia, et cetera. We must learn to talk to each other, they say, before we can have a stern chat with capitalism.

This is frustrating for a Marxist. And *not* because a Marxist does not seek to end precisely those forms of divisive social organization. We have long sought to end them. We Marxists say, "Freedom for each is freedom for all," and we really mean it — there's no Thomas Jefferson–style clause in there that excludes non-whites or non-males. Marx and his patron and collaborator Friedrich Engels — especially Engels, who was a bit of a bachelor lad — had no belief in the naturalness of the family: the unit that has given and continues to give so much pain to so many women. We Marxists believe we must unite to change the mode of production so that we can change social division.

Yes, and again, fuck *yes*, we Marxists *despise* division. We seek a world in which the lives of each and all are unencumbered by too much work, too much alienation, and too little time to lay about wondering what we each might like to do. We are at pains to understand how cultural and identity discrimination forms and is spread. We say that it's not *all* down to the forces and relations of production — what we call "the base" — but that these are always are least half the conversation. They are always present, so please let's quit pretending that the people's heads can be cleaned without us first sanitizing the dirty backdrop of capitalism.

The base informs culture and identity and all the sometimes wonderful but usually terrible stuff that we Marxists call the "superstructure." The superstructure talks back to the base. The base listens. But the base predominates; it has the first and last word. Even the great critic Walter Benjamin agrees that crude material things are the "things without which no refined and spiritual things could exist." And that fucker just loved his culture.

The basest way of talking about the base is that there is no way to assert your culture and identity if you don't have enough sandwiches to survive. I cannot explore what it means to be queer, for example, without pastrami on rye. *Yes*, with sauerkraut, thanks, comrade. I'm surprised you had to ask.

If you think the superstructure produces the base, then you are, unfortunately for the workers' revolution, not yet a Marxist. If you think that we can change all the laws and words and cultural sensitivities first, and the base will *then* fall into place, then you have turned Marx upside down to become near identical with the liberal philosophies he spent his life upturning.

That's okay. You can believe that what comes first for a truly good life is favorable speech and enhanced sensitivity and empowering television programs. You can believe that figures like Amy Schumer or Solange Knowles will tell enough jokes and sing sufficient notes that we'll all be inspired as feminists and then go on to see the logic of a collectively owned material world … just know that if you think this, you are not a Marxist. Sure, you can call yourself one. Call yourself whatever you fancy. But know that Marx wrote this whole superstructure-base interrelation down, and if you want to turn it into something that suits you, you don't really need to bother reading Marx. He is, let me tell you, a complicated nightmare to endure. *Capital* is no fun at all to read. Spare yourself the trouble and have a good night's sleep before transforming the culture, in the vain hope that this act will transform the base.

I am serious about this. If you don't think that you can agree with this sandwich part of Marx, don't bother finding out if you're a Marxist. Because the only way to truly know if you're a Marxist is to truly read Marx and, FFS, I truly wish I didn't have to. It's hard. And long. Sometimes it makes me sleepy. Then, it wakes me up again when I see it through Marx's eyes.

Even Marx himself expressed to many correspondents that he would rather be doing something else. Neither of us wanted to do this criticism-of-capitalism thing. We'd both much rather be drunk and going on about culture. Do you think I *enjoy* trying to understand the tendency of the rate of profit to fall (Chapter 13 of Volume 3 of *Capital*)? No. I'd rather poke myself in the tit with a fork. But, as capitalism keeps poking me in the tit with a fork anyway, I figure, what the dang? I'm in my late forties and shall probably die quite soon. So, before I am found cold with the prongs of oppressive capitalist flatware lodged deep within my bosom, it is my single hope that I can convince some of those persons who identify as progressive that it all *begins with the base.* Not *it all begins with me* or it all begins with Amy Schumer getting her politics on point before uttering a dirty but morally pure joke. There are no good conversations about culture and identity without a good sandwich first. A starving comrade cannot discuss the nature of gendered pronouns.

This is not to gracelessly say that the discussion of gendered pronouns is one not worth having. It absolutely is. This is not a case of "Whataboutery," such as we might have heard as children from our parents. "What about the children starving in Africa," they say, when we refuse to eat our quinoa. We grow up and hear it again as adults. People insist that while there are those with no food, we in the West must simply accept all forms of cultural torture. We must not worry about whether you can use a particular bathroom or replace a "he" with "them," they say. As I am not an actual bastard, I do not join these people in saying that your struggle is nothing when there are "true struggles" at play. Your bathroom struggle is a legitimate struggle. The "What about" tactic is one advanced *so often* by conservatives, who will take up traditionally Leftist causes like poverty or LGBTI rights or feminism for women in the Middle East whenever it suits them.

I am not urging you to be less "politically correct." I am urging you femmos to see the interweaving of the base and the superstructure. I am urging you to see that the one thing that unites every worker on the planet is their enslavement to capital — not just the money or asset that helps build investment, but the building block of social relations as we presently know them. I am *not* urging you to a match of "Whataboutery." "You think that's bad, well what about THIS?" Fuck that. I want no part of such teatime conversation. Let's leave this low sport to the right-wing racist ass-cactus who is suddenly a psychic gender theory scholar when there's a Muslim chick around. It's all, "I'm pretty sure you don't want to wear that nasty hob-job, let's rip it off," followed by some fake transnational feminism in the form of, "Western women will not help you. But I will," before sodding off to his church where there is not now, nor ever will there be, female clergy.

This game of "What about" is *old*. It's been around as long as there've been people to play it, which is to say for the entire history of liberalism. In the nineteenth century, Lord Cromer, ruler of British-occupied Egypt, urged for the unveiling of Muslim women, despite having been a founding member of the Men's League for Opposing Women's Suffrage in England. He said he wanted to alleviate the oppression of Egyptian Muslim women. Got real interested in the ladies' freedom the minute he sensed that by these means he could deny it. "I am freeing you by taking from you the most visible symbol of your identity." Gee, thanks, First Earl of Racist Hypocrites.

His act was to promote disunity, comrades, as I'm sure you need not be told. What Marxism seeks to do under capitalism is to reunify us all as workers. We, the producers of things and of actions, are bound together. There are those folks who see this kind of unity as a sort of undernuanced knot.

*Nuance*. There's a word that's used a lot these days. "That's not a very nuanced argument," or, "You just don't *get* nuance," are two reproaches I see all over the shop. It is not *nuanced* of you to consider that not all women have a vagina. It is not *nuanced* of you to consider that not all women can do without lip gloss. Not just in feminism — but everywhere we hear the urgent need for "nuance." It is as though we have begun to believe that we can fix the world only through first knowing the personal history of each of its inhabitants.

People use the term "nuance" negatively to describe its absence in big things, like a government department or a Marxist understanding. They use it positively to describe its presence in smaller things, like a single person or group.

I'm not saying it's a silly word, or that it is always a stupid charge to make. It is *true* that there is much understanding that lacks "nuance." I, for example, lack nuance in my understanding of twentieth-century visual art as much as I do in the cultural practice of people in the Trobriand Islands. If I were to hold forth on either of these (and, let's be frank, most other) matters, you'd be right to say that I lacked nuance, and should certainly shut my trap.

"Lack of nuance" is a criticism you can apply to knowledge that depends on fine-grain detail. But it's not a really useful criticism to make of the big things in the world. Or even quite large institutions. It seems to me to be a little dim to say, "That bank lacks nuance." Anything that employs and buys so many is bound to be bound up in rules.

This is not to say that Marxism is bound up in "rules." What Marxism is bound up in, as I do hope I've explained, is a dynamic way of thinking about the dynamic system of capitalism. And it is not, for a minute, to say that that big system is simple itself. (Marx himself spent a lifetime describing the complex and dominating behavior of capital, when all he really wanted to do was drink wine and read entertaining novels.) It *is* to say that "nuance" is not the gateway to full understanding that many suppose it to be.

"Your argument lacks nuance," is a phrase I have often read and heard used to convey disagreement. Personally, I would prefer to hear, "Your argument is bullshit." The idea that all the little nuanced details can add up to a single revolutionary truth is perplexing to me, although it is very popular in the present; particularly in feminist media, so very full of nuanced personal stories.

There is this prevalent idea, particularly among prevalent women, that if we only carve out space for everyone to speak, nuance will arrive and rescue our movement from being what it has been for so very long: a bunch of straight rich white girls chiefly interested in being the first to hit that glass ceiling.

*The glass ceiling.* I would, I think, vow to keep my pussy empty for a year if I could be promised a liberal feminist conversation that did not point to this architectural surface. To say that there is a ceiling, even if it is one that needs to be smashed by a courageous few, is to accept the idea of ascent without question.

Even in less obviously capitalist scenarios, the fight is so often for one of ascent. This happens in feminism, as it does in other identity politics movements. When, in 2016, the fairly middling intellectual Lionel Shriver gave a fairly middling speech at the Brisbane Writer's Festival, she made headlines around the world for her attack on what is called "cultural appropriation." Shriver felt she should be "allowed" to write about anything she wanted. The young liberal activist Yassmin Abdel-Magied was offended by this claim. She was also, I imagine, cheesed by the picture Shriver was painting of an army of "politically correct" others out to prevent the lauded author from writing about people from cultures with which she was not especially familiar. Abdel-Magied had a point, as an individual. She was, in my view, correct to point out that it was so difficult for Muslim women — so long "freed" into compulsory worship of Western traditions to save them from their own — to carve out a space. But, we must look at the nature of the space that is being contested. It is not the space of everyday speech. It is not a fight for everyday people. It is a fight for authors and others paid to speak at literary festivals.

This is not to suggest that Abdel-Magied had no point to make. I will admit, begrudgingly, that Shriver, *such* an average thinker, made half a point when she said that everyone was obsessed with the "right" to preserve the nuances of their identity these days. It is to say, first, that the matter of cultural dominance cannot be contested when material dominance is not. (It's no coincidence that the nation that holds the world's reserve currency is also the nation that inflicts its culture upon the world.) It is to say, second, that there will only ever be a few people invited to literary festivals, and the power that they hold on that stage does not trickle down to others.

We all know that not everyone is going to get to the top, right? Even when the glass ceiling is busted, what implicitly remains is the fact of the climb to the top. Until organizations are collectively owned and managed, as they will be in a truly communist mode of production, there can only ever be a few owners and managers of a firm or a government department.

Why should I, a laborer of very modest means, care to be the meal for a lioness? If a woman stands on my worker's shoulders, then later writes a bestselling autobiography where she claims to be the giant on whose shoulders all history's women have stood, what's in it for me, and her and her and her? Other than a really boring afternoon of instruction on how to "lean in" to a system of success. One that rewards "merit" and leaves us to suppose that there are simply some people with qualities inborn who deserve more — which is a form of social organization that has *precisely* the shape of sexism.

I *do* understand what's in it for us ladies at an emotional level. When we women read books, *so many* books, and countless status updates by successful women, we feel temporarily bold. These women tell us "relatable" stories in which they, too, felt the pain of the male gaze, or the fear of being plump, but turned their fear and pain into anger and, then, right into success. In these stories by women, for women, and about women, we see the conflation of two systems, which are not at all "nuanced." First, we have the everyday story of the women, who all suffer under patriarchy. Then, we see patriarchy stared down with the force of capitalist and/or celebrity success. So *many* feminist women are quite unabashed in their quest for great wealth and power. They say, "I love money," or, "I love to inspire others," so rarely examining the fact that their money and their power to inspire are contingent on a system that denies it to so many others.

Under the capitalist mode of production, and the capitalist mode of thought, freedom for a few only results in the delusion of freedom for all.

I am not asking those of you who enjoy your charismatic power or the power of your money to feel bad. I am asking you to examine the claims of "I'm worth it!" we see so often. Of course you are "worth it," because everybody is, as the Marxist agrees. So, let's make sure that everybody on the planet who's "worth it," which is everybody, gets their due: a good life.

You do not give those others a good life by giving up your own right now. Feel no guilt. (Unless you work in the finance sector, natch.) You are not directly responsible for the fact that others, just as "worth it" as you, are deemed to have no value. But if you continue to be feminist without examining the role of capitalism in the lives of every woman, you will do only very little for very few. And if you counter this with, "Well, I'm happy if it helps just one person," good on ya, love. I'm not. I consider helping just one person a great underachievement.

The other week, I was reading a typical woman's plight: "How do I earn a living and take care of my children?" The glib answer here is, "Fight for a communist mode of production, in which we are all unlikely to work much more than ten hours a week." Simplistic, but true. The real-world capitalism answer a Marxist would give — we *do* compromise, and you wouldn't have an eight-hour work day if we hadn't — is more like, "We must fight for all families to have affordable access to childcare of the very highest quality, no matter their wage."

For me, the question of having a child at all was answered by capitalism. The income on which I have tolerably lived through most of my childbearing years answered for me: no. Anything that I had to say about the matter "as a woman" was secondary. And don't give me, "You could make it work if you really wanted." First, my eggs are probably fried by now. Second, who would be watching my costly IVF baby that I cannot afford while I read *Capital*, somewhat perversely, for profit? And, jeez, I'm one of the lucky ones. I earn the median wage. If AUD$50K a year doesn't cut it for a single parent, then a woman who works in retail on several thousand fewer dollars should probably sell her uterus.

Sometimes, in these ubiquitous feminist discussions, matters of capitalism are explicitly discussed. Questions about the gender pay gap, for example, are posed. The answers are sometimes quite good and grind down to another good question: Why do we pay so little in health care and retail, sectors of large female employment?

Then, invariably, comes a bad answer. Or, at least, an incomplete one. The answer is, "Because they're female jobs, silly." Well, yes and no. They are also jobs under capitalism and capitalism demands that there are those employees who will, whatever their gender, work more cheaply.

You may recall that feminist icon Hillary Clinton said in a semiprivate speech that there were those who were "baristas," spat out as though it were a slur. For this stark bigotry, may she never buy a coffee in the continental United States again. Why should baristas, gods on whose miracles I depend, be considered less valuable than dentists, also providers of miracles? All work is valuable. (Well, apart from that shit that involves the accumulation of capital. You highly paid finance industry people can suck it. And, no. I don't feel bad saying this, because the minute you screw us workers by preying on our need for credit, you'll be saved by a bailout. Dry your tears with the TARP bill, you scum.)

Via media outlets, liberal feminism currently delivers us a great volume of first-person accounts of struggle under sexism. My body shame. My encounter with sexism at work. My bad time at the café with my baby carriage. I mean, I get it at an emotional level. I do. But the way in which these stories must be resolved, even by the fact of their telling, is a terrible lie. The author survives. The author thrives, at least to the degree that she has her account of trauma widely viewed.

What even *is* that, when women think they can show patriarchy a thing or two through the capitalist acquisition of money or renown? *Yes, I suffered a brutal moment of sexism, but I got even by starting a homemade preserve empire!* As though this were a solution available to every one of my sisters who has suffered the atrocity of rape. Fix the crimes of the patriarchy with a big dose of capitalism? This seems to me like treating stage-four brain cancer with a fatal head injury. Then again, I do lack "nuance."

Peoples' lives are full of nuance, of course. A very common complaint by feminists, and other activists whose chief interest is the social advancement of a particular identity group, is that in Marxism, "nuance" is lacking. We Marxists don't see, say some feminists, the specificity of the feminine experience. Ergo, without nuance, we can never hope to have a revolution that truly includes women.

I will say that Marxism, as it has been practiced, has lacked not just nuance but basic fucking sense when it comes to my gender. But I will also say that the capitalist mode of production, the object of Marx's critique, lacks "nuance" as well.

Sure, capitalism produces many different commodities and engages every person, all of them nuanced, on the planet. But yelling at a big complex to be more "nuanced" makes about as much sense as, I don't know, asking Solange to be less cool. Or, better, asking the bank to really *get* who you are inside when you apply for refinancing. The bank may commission advertisements showing a diverse group of potential borrowers having warm conversations with the loans officer. You may even meet a cool loans officer who actually does care to really get who you are inside. But the bank is not in the business of any understanding of you more intimate than your ability to service a loan.

Banks don't profit from "nuance." They profit from making a cold assessment of capitalism.

There is a view that many feminist people have that Marxism simply doesn't make room for women and is not a way of thinking that can, if applied, hope to address the problem of what we call "the patriarchy." Just to be gracelessly clear about this: you're right. Marxism is a criticism of capitalism and not one of patriarchy. If you're looking for that One Weird Trick to fix all the problems of the planet, the terrible news is it doesn't and couldn't exist.

Those close pals, capitalism and patriarchy, have been photographed in company by some non-Marxist feminists. The liberal feminist says that capitalism is bad only because it makes her feel bad about her body. The Left-liberal feminist might tell capitalism it is bad only because it makes her buy things she doesn't need. But, there are some feminists who have seized upon a more genuinely nuanced way to conflate these two, and other, detrimental systems.

I do understand why the thing we now call "intersectionality" evolved. It was a useful resistance against the smugness of white folk. It came from black and brown people, some of them from the academic school we call "critical race theory." In a sophisticated effort to ensure their lives were considered for the very first time in social movements and theory that had for so long been written by whites, for whites, and about whites, people black and brown said, "Let's put *everyone* in our oppression atlas." Honestly, I think this was very generous. I imagine that if I were a black or brown person, the temptation to simply tell white people to fuck off would be irresistible.

This intersectionality thing can be thought of as a road map. In fact, the scholar who really established the word describes those roads. Kimberlé Crenshaw wrote, in 2001:

> Intersectionality is what occurs when a woman from a minority group ... tries to navigate the main crossing in the city ... The main highway is "Racism Road." One crossroad can be Colonialism, then Patriarchy Street ... She has to deal not only with one form of

oppression but with all forms, those named as road signs which link together to make a double, a triple, a multiple, a many layered blanket of oppression.

Leaving aside that Crenshaw could have gone with "overpasses of oppression" rather than blankets, which are not often known to intersect, this analysis looks at first quite good. It certainly looks good to many feminists in the present. They say, "This solves it all! There's so much *nuance*." Intersectionality thinks about people, especially women people, in a matrix. Each little dot represents an individual who is subject to different negative forces within the shared social space. Sometimes, in this 3D visualization, she will encounter just one sort of nonsense, and at others, a big old soggy rug of oppression will hit her as she's crossing Sizeism Boulevard.

There are, for the Marxist, a few problems with this very popular analysis. We'll get to these. But, first I will say again that the move by intersectional scholars and activists to include all marginal groups in the cultural conversation was both gracious and good. What I won't offer is that very common critique, that the problem with intersectionality is that it's a game of Oppression Olympics, akin to a round of "Whataboutery."

I don't mind if a handful of people have a whine about how rotten their lives are. Sometimes we need to hear that. And, even if they can be, in rare times, said to be playing up their oppression achievement, who cares? Everybody's always whining about something. This includes rich white men who complain that their "freedom of speech" is curtailed by the fact that they are now forced to read novels written by black women in their expensive, formerly all-white all-male universities. And this obviously also includes me. I'll whip out my wandering sexual preferences at appropriate times, just as I will weaponize any little thing about my life that will help me make a case in an argument, or get out of jail, or whatever.

Sometimes I express my identity as powerless Helen who is too poor to have a baby. Sometimes I am powerful Helen who once worked for the *Sydney Morning Herald*. When, for example, in the company of posh white elites, I may hint at a past professional credential, such as working at one of the nation's old newspapers. When in the company of my intersectional sisters, I might remind them that their handout on the "oppression matrix" is printed in a typeface too small for this blind lady to see. By accentuating my status as a winner or a loser, I seek to win these exchanges either way.

We experience our identities all the time. We all talk about our identities, or subtly emphasize different facets of them, all the time. *I am very Australian. I am very global. I am very educated. I am very working class.* If you have genuinely learned the trick of engaging with others with no trace of consciousness about your identity, I would like to know your secret. I would pay you in gold.

As intersectional scholars and activists sensibly point out, the only people who feel truly emptied of identity are those who are the least bothered by it. Which is to say, well-to-do white chaps. It is no mere coincidence that these are the persons most eager to say, "I don't see color," or, "Women would get a lot further if they stopped complaining about being women so much." As their identities are the dominant, and therefore default, type, they can proceed more easily with a lot of self-deluded rot about how "science" and "reason" and "free speech" are the only things that matter. "Come join us in this Enlightenment club that we built, whose signs banning Jews and Irish we took down as long ago as last February. We are reasonable men who care not for your petty claims that it's hard to be you. Make my coffee, there's a doll."

*White* is an identity, even if it seems to some like a free pass to pretend that this "identity" crap means nothing, and "What are you whining about, you exotic lass?" Actually, many racist nationalist types now even openly claim their whiteness as an identity. The so-called "identitarian" movement now forms part of the US alt-right. It is interesting to note that this bowel movement started in France, a nation that really gave us the idea of the "citizen," and her associated "rights," in 1789; a nation that has, since that time, produced a lot of work on the "self." And, yes, I'm looking at you, Michel Foucault. You fucker.

If you see that there may be some common territory of thought for the racist identitarian and the anti-racist intersectional scholar, can't say as I disagree with you. While many scholars and activists, including Audre Lorde — who, since her death, has been retrofitted with the label "intersectional" — came at the discipline in an effort to get white people to shut up for a minute, we can trace some of its genealogy back to France.

This is not to suggest that brown and black people are not entirely capable of producing their own knowledge and theory. It is to say, however, that intersectionality is a method of thinking that did *itself* intersect with white Western thought traditions from the time of its birth. And, NO, I am not saying that intersectionality is white on the inside. Actually, I think it's capitalist on the inside.

Again. Cultural oppression is real. As I am able to stay indoors and write my life away, I don't experience much of it myself, but I know that it can be very keenly felt. Brown and black people, disabled people, and people with a nonnormative gender experience cop some extraordinary shit. It's real. The cultural experience is real, and it is not, as we have discussed at length, simply the result of the way we organize labor. But, all of these experiences can be linked to the base. Yet the intersectionalist says, much in the way the identitarian does, that there is some kind of identity "essence." Something that precedes the experience of capitalism.

Okay. Right. Things get tricky here, and we need to talk a little feminist theory. Yes, gender precedes capitalism. The idea of woman as the material and man as the ideal has existed in Western culture for thousands of years. It is our oldest and most stable social division.

There are two major ways feminist people have come to understand this fact. First, and most currently popular, is the idea we can see in the work of Judith Butler. That is: biological sex is simply gender's alibi, that we *do* gender and it is not naturally received. Second, is that gender and sex are indivisible. We are just "born that way" and what we do in the world is simply an expression of the natural.

As I am accustomed to argument, I prefer to go for an unpopular third option, which is to not think the question "Are our gender expressions natural?" important at all. Whatever the answer, we'll never know, so there is zero imperative to give a fuck. I do suspect, per psychoanalytic feminism (yes, it's mostly French), that for as long as sexual biological differences are evident to children, children will grow into adults with a sense of the "binary" so despised by fans of Butler. Short of every male and female couple — who have the frustrating habit of living together in large numbers and making babies — wearing elaborate masks, this difference will be bound to reproduce itself. I suspect that there will, for some time, be a sense of the division: both from oneself and the primary caregiver, as one moves from infancy to childhood; and between "two sorts of people," which most people learn early to schematize as male and as female. Machines may change all of this in the future.

But in the meantime, we are unlikely to change this soon in meaningful numbers, because most of us work long hours and don't have time to convey to our children a psychoanalytic theory of the self. So, sue me, I think two primary categories of gender, by which all others are compared, are, for the foreseeable future, inevitable. You can no-platform me for being transphobe if you like. But I am not prescribing behavior. I am merely describing the acquisition of identity itself as it occurs.

Which takes us back to Marx's part-time buddy, Aristotle, who says that we are, by nature, social. It's true. We prematurely born mammals *need* people throughout our childhoods, and continue to desire them all our lives. Our survival, first material and then emotional, will always depend on others. Which is why, sisters, you need some more Marx in your feminism diet.

We are stuck here together. We need time and space to explore all of time and space. One of its most fascinating, troubling questions, for people everywhere, will long continue to be sex and gender. How do we do it better? How do we let it not overwhelm us with its possibly inevitable strictures? And, jeez, what would it look like under communism?

Probably, for quite some time, just as bad as it does now. Of course, women would no longer be financially dependent on individual men. Women who seek refuge from men who beat them will not be consigned to a shelter, but move to something much better than a safe house: a place to live. Women in poor health or in need of reproductive guidance will not have to travel and skimp to find it. Women will not worry that they cannot afford to have their babies cared for and may very well elect to pop them with a service when needed as they pursue their own productive acts and free time.

Then, a few decades in, women may worry that this division of labor is something that is itself reproducing "binary" tendencies in their children. They will talk about it with others. They will think about it. They will write about a better way. They will be talking less about who gets to do the keynote address at a literary festival and more about the poetry of the everyday. Perhaps, if they have produced some thought that excites others, they will even recite this at a literary festival, where we all gather to remember the olden times in which well-to-do ladies filled the content management systems of privately held companies with advice only for the tiny ruling class.

We will still hurt each other. We will still bicker. We will judge other women and men. We are, being human, very far from perfect, and this will be no utopia. It will be the only place, however, where we are all able to deliver our very *nuanced* understandings of each other. There will be peace, and long hours for us to ask what it does mean, can mean and has meant to be female, male, gender-nonconforming, or even gender-jaded.

**6**

---

# "OMG" And "What The Fudge"!! What Do We Even Do Now?

---

**M**arx, as you may agree, provides some critical tools to set us free. He also gives us great cause to be fucking miserable. Those are some *big* thoughts he's got, and the weight of them has sometimes led me to moments of depressed, confused paralysis. In these last pages, I want to try to spare you such a mood. I'm going to do this first by being briefly and truly miserable about the enormity of the transformative task Marx has left us with. I'm then going to suggest ways in which you can take your miserable new Marxism out for an uplifting walk in the mean streets of capitalism. I am going to attempt to answer the question I am sure has formed in your mind. Which is, "That's all very nice, Helen, but what is to be done?"

Okay.

Since reading Marx, the popular phrase "bleeding heart Leftie" has perplexed me. If there's a hemorrhage taking place after an afternoon with *Capital*, it's not in my heart but my brain. Yes, we're "bleeding hearts" and *of course* we are agreed that it is morally wrong for people to suffer exploitation, alienation, war, bigotry, and those other disorders brought forth or refined by the capitalist mode of production. Our problem is not a lack of compassion. Honestly, I think most people, *even* neoliberals, have oodles of compassion and must go to great lengths to conceal it from themselves; it takes unnatural effort to pretend that others deserve less than you do. Our problem is the size and the influence of the system described in such detail by Marx. It's a *headache*.

This thing — a big set of social relations that extends far beyond everyday material life and gets into the very stuff of *us* — is so hard to see past. Think of the way even a moderate socialist like Bernie Sanders is ridiculed as a fantasist for suggesting that the planet's richest nation can afford to send its young people to university at no cost to the student. Think of the way that Jeremy Corbyn has been pilloried for reviving the mid-century aims of his Labour Party, which are as simple as greater income equality. Think of the way that the phrase "Too big to fail" fell so easily into our vernacular, as though without financial institutions of monumental size and fictitious "productivity," everything would suddenly stop.

It is easier for us to imagine plagues of zombies, alien invasion, or utter nuclear devastation than it is to imagine the end of capitalism. Even if we do begin to imagine a world in which there is no private property — the aim of the Marxist, in case you missed it — there is generally someone around to tell us that we're being stupid or immoral. Or even someone we know well who kindly reminds us that what we're trying to envision is a chimera. A very bright friend of mine, whose opinion I respect on all matters that are not economic, says to me during our frequent arguments, "But, Helen, growth is the natural way of things. We have children and we hope for them to have better than we did," and he repeats this to me as an incontrovertible truth. Capitalism is the natural expression of human nature, he tells me. We're doing it for the kids.

Although I am not a parent, I very much share his sense of moral responsibility. Which is to say, as much as I despise the music and the memes of Millennials, I also consider it an obligation to clean up this stinking latrine of a planet for their future use. I *do* want to offer them better, and not because I am a nice or honorable person — clearly I am not — but because what the fuck am I doing here after billions of years of wonderful evolutionary accidents if not agitating for something more sustainable?

Perhaps if I had just one child and did not conceive of myself as the mother of many I will never meet, I might feel otherwise. However, I suspect not. The better thing I'd wish for my own child is her freedom, which is, for a Marxist, contingent on freedom for all. I wish that all for you, my young comrades. I don't even have to *like* you to want this very badly for you. You don't have to like others to want it for them. You can certainly feel at your liberty to dislike me, if you prefer. Honestly, I really loathed the person who introduced me to the headache that is Marx, so

I wouldn't be surprised. But, if you are committed to the thing you may call by names as various as "social justice" or "income equality" or "inclusion," you *must* examine the ideas of a man who insists that the free development of each is the condition for the free development of all.

As I point out to my friend, the policy settings that delivered better conditions to successive generations were limited to particular places and eras. In Western nations, this has roughly been since the middle of the nineteenth century to the middle of the twentieth — and even these fleeting benefits, felt in nations like Australia and the USA, were largely offered only to persons with pale skin. At all other times and in all other places, things have been shithouse under this purportedly wonderful system. Now, they're shithouse in the West, too. If you are young now, you are likely aware that the chances your material riches will exceed those of your parents are zilch.

This is the era, then, for those who are prepared to fight, not just for yourselves, but for your own children. Which is when I stop being miserable and forget about my bright friend who maintains his powerful, almost religious delusion that capitalism is natural and inevitable, because I can see a new generation of people who realize that it is neither. Let's talk about what *they* can do, and, first, how they are uniquely placed to do it.

Millennials are, potentially, a great revolutionary force. First, many of them have inherited the useful parts of so-called "identity politics" and so have a basic understanding that their experience of the world does not precisely match everybody else's — they know that racism is an everyday burden that some bear, and others do not. Second, many of them have acquired what we call class consciousness. It would be quite difficult to be young in this era and *not* sense that the greater part of your effort, both in leisure and in work, is in the service of somebody else's profit.

So, there are a group of kids as frustrated with the intolerance of cultural difference as they are with their own exclusion from a capitalist society's false promises. Unlike their Leftist Boomer predecessors, who enjoyed relative abundance, they face the very real possibility of poverty. The Boomer, back then, did not see poverty as a true problem, and began to focus on purely liberal concerns like cultural intolerance, racism, sexism, et cetera. The Leftist Boomer saw capitalism as relatively benign. It's often said that the Leftists of the mid-twentieth century gave up on economics and offered all their attention to the problems of the culture — this is often called in Marxist writing "the Cultural Turn."

Young Leftists, however, see the problems of cultural and economic inequality as interwoven. For this reason, they are, in my crusty old opinion, poised to become more authentically Marxist than any previous generation.

I give "awareness raising" a lot of shit. I have often written about my frustration with, for example, the sort of Clintonista who sees only sisterhood, to the exclusion of class. You know the sort of thing: the persistent liberal belief that if we celebrate a woman of color making it to the c-suites of Silicon Valley, her victory will trickle down to all.

I have no doubt that this particular woman fought hard to attain her position. But, it is important for us Marxists to remember that she is no longer of our class. It is a false solidarity to celebrate these achievements.

I see kids knowing that the mark of a truly free society is not the elevation of a woman of color to the capitalist class. But, they also know that the mark of a freedom-seeking movement is not the *exclusion* of a woman of color. They see both that cultural difference must be accepted as an inevitable fact of human life, and that class solidarity of the 99 percent, whatever their cultural differences, is a precondition for social change.

Now, what is *not* a precondition for social change is to become a thoroughly orthodox Marxist. There are problems with Marx and there are some elements of his thinking that are necessarily tied to the nineteenth century. If you do further reading, you'll find that, for example, the labor theory of value has been rejected or modified by some people who still proudly call themselves twenty-first-century Marxists. You'll find that his ideas on ideology have been significantly updated. You'll find, perhaps, that what became at times his thoroughly scientific approach to human social history fails — we're complicated beasts who will probably always remain a bit of a mystery to ourselves, especially when we get together, as we inevitably must. That's our whole deal as humans. We need each other to survive, and in our interactions a great deal of complexity not always fully grasped by Marx — or any thinker ever — can arise.

Marx is not perfect. However, his account of capitalism, now so neglected in our universities and media, is one with which it is, for anyone committed to the ideas of freedom and quality, vital to engage. To ignore this critique is to ignore the vastness of capitalism.

Marx is capitalism's constant shadow. He was not the architect of the failed Soviet experiment or any other of the examples of state capitalism. He did not provide a blueprint for communism. He provided an account of the ways in which capitalism produces a particular reality. It is only within Marx and Marxism that what we have thought previously to be our relationship with the truth of the modern world reveals itself as just another perspective. He's the guy that made it possible for us to stand outside ourselves for a while. Even if you retain your faith in the idea of privately held property, you can still afford to philosophically engage with Marx in this "outsider" way.

What you who have urgent concerns for the future cannot afford to do, in my partial view, is fail to give Marx some time. This is my single recommendation.

I do understand that you want to know what to do right now. We have, for good reason, a sense of approaching a limit. There's a bag of circus peanuts in the White House. There's a bunch of people publicly screeching about "free speech" but doing their best to make sure that their free speech is never freely contested. Our media are centrally owned. Our friends are resorting to hashtags and boycotts and telling us that all the world needs now is "compassion," when we can see that it's going to take a lot more than that to address the environmental, economic, cultural, and social problems of our planet. There are plenty of people suggesting single solutions to these complex questions. Marxism may not answer these questions outright. But, it certainly identifies many of the right questions to ask.

So, this is your answer: find more problems. If you're the kind of chap, like me, who frets for our future, allow your thinking to be problematized by Marx. Take the risk and try for a diagnosis before applying a cure. Use the instruments of Marxism to learn what ails the social body, and what can revive it. And, yes, I know these are not satisfying answers and it would be better to end this book with the declaration of a state of emergency and an exhortation to act NOW. But, the terrible news is, you have to think before you act.

And by *you*, I mean Millennials. With unfeigned respect for my generation, you and I must concede that we're done. We have failed to uphold the promise of the true Left, which is Marx's historical materialist Left, and we are set in our liberal ways. When Margaret Thatcher, one of the early purveyors of the thing we call neoliberalism — which is simply a return to the classical economic liberalism that Marx refuted — said, "There is No Alternative," we did not meaningfully counter her. We turned our attention only to winning cultural battles and let her claim economic victory. We, being then still quite comfortable in the West, forgot the idea for which others had died: that the idea and the material interweave.

We do not win the cultural battles for equality, diversity, inclusion or whatever you'd like to call it without also doing battle with political economy. We do not win the trust of potential comrades by writing smug, hideous remarks about "stupid" Trump voters. When we forget that neoliberalism — again, basically a return to classical models of economic thinking, after a brief historical period of the crisis-aware thinking called Keynesianism — is also stupid, we lose. We have lost in this period.

So, dear fellow Western Gen X-er, you and I — both as the result of our failure to do anything but promote "cultural understanding" and of our advanced age — can do little but catch up on our Marxist reading. This is our penance for wasting our youth in unwitting service to neoliberal policy. We are not permitted to grumble about The Youth but we are required, if we retain our interest in a better future, to support their efforts. And these efforts are destined to be, as all efforts toward a post-capitalist world have hitherto been, fumbling. But, let's take responsibility. We've put true Leftism on hold for all our lives. We have contributed almost nothing to this long conversation. You and I have been going on for so long about such total shit — our need to "express" ourselves, our need to declare our marvelous, borderless fluid identities, our self-esteem, our need to be heard — that we must now fall into silence.

Which means, dear Millennial, that I can't tell you what to do. I reckon it's okay to give you a very simplified overview of Marx as I understand him, and I figure it's okay to remind you of the lessons my generation forgot. I figure it's okay to remind you that true communism cannot be declared a disaster, because it has *never been tried.*

I figure it's okay to provoke you into a little communist muddle. What would this world look like? Could it be a truly free place where the state eventually withers away after a period of transition, or will it require some limited authority in place to address history's greatest threats — nuclear weapons and environmental devastation — both problems created and then never solved by capitalism? How much deliberation should a person like to engage in? Do you want a future where you are required to talk about roads, childcare, the allocation of land to live on, or do you want to leave this to others? How will we appoint the architects of the future, and how do we stop them becoming haughty, dangerous technocrats? How will we address, or even define, crime? What will we do with all our free time?!

It's okay to nudge you into questions. It's not okay to give you the answers. Other than the reminder to unite!!!!! Even when you don't particularly agree about a lot of other stuff!!!!!!!!!!!!!!!! You, the 99 percent, have 100 percent of the world to win. Go get it.

# Further Reading and Viewing, Comrade

I f you have not, by now, been coaxed by boredom into a zombie capitalist state where you'd prefer to live on intravenous LIES instead of the socialist truth, I have some suggestions for you.

BTW, I know many of you would prefer a plan for revolution to a reading list, but if it ain't obvious at this point that I think that thinking is just as important as acting, and, indeed, must immediately precede any act of revolution in order to ensure its effectiveness, well. I guess I have been less explicit and rude about my entire "Become a part of the vanguard and read a fucking book!" message than I think.

I would like to say that before you read Marx — and, you oughta — you should know that me, her, and Hooziwhatsit

Marxists don't accept all of his ideas uncritically. For example, the labor theory of value is one highly problematized idea. Which you will find if you read the popular text *A Companion to Marx's Capital* by David Harvey. Orthodox Marxists, and even people like me who approach Marx in a more artsy-fartsy way, have difficulty letting the idea of the surplus provided by the worker go. But, it seems pretty slippery in Harvey's work. I still think he provides a good introduction — and you can also look at his lectures on YouTube.

Another guy who is "problematic" (jeez, I loathe that word. Why don't people just say what they mean, which is "disagreeable" or "wrong") is Slavoj Žižek. I would recommend *The Sublime Object of Ideology* and *Violence*. A load of people will tell you that Žižek is a Marxist joke who courts popular attention. As though jokes or attention are bad things. Look. I really like him, and not only because he is clownish and often accessible. I disagree with his recent pronouncements that dialectical materialism (pretty much the same thing as historical materialism, don't worry about it) is a tool best left in the nineteenth century, but I love his efforts to reconcile a theory of psychoanalysis with a theory of capitalism. You can watch heaps of his videos on the internet. You can see lots of turdy things written by people who misunderstand him, and a few great critiques by those who understand him, but still disagree. Either way, he is an entertaining route into Marxism. He is a gateway drug.

There are loads of contemporary economists and political economists who are not really Marxist, but damn useful nonetheless. I am an enormous fan of Mark Blyth, whose *Austerity: History of a Bad Idea* is, genuinely, one of the best popular explanations of neoliberalism for which a girl could hope. The Australian economist Steve Keen — a guy who predicted the GFC — has a book called *Debunking Economics* but it is way too technical for mine. Still, Steve is a great person to follow on social media and a real little fucker who sticks it to status quo economists. He is also extraordinarily generous with his time and answers the questions from all and sundry via his various accounts. Ann Pettifor is a fabulously cranky lady and I always enjoy her lectures, although I haven't read *The Production of Money*. Friends tell me it is great. And Michael Hudson — reportedly, Trotsky's godson — wrote a marvy thing called *Killing the Host*.

The very famous economist, and former finance minister of Greece, Yanis Varoufakis does some hot shit lectures. I gave his *The Global Minotaur* a go, but it was too wet with analogy for my taste. You might like it. If not, many of his speeches — again, available on YouTube — are wonderful, especially "Confessions of an Erratic Marxist." I find he as at his best in offering an ongoing account of things as they are, rather than a grand narrative, which a person like Žižek, or Blyth, is so skilled in providing. But, both Žižek and Blyth are more philosophers than economists, and the former is my personal preference. You may be more of a numbers girl. I am a bit more fartsy, as mentioned.

Be careful with the economists you choose to entertain. Look for their liberalism and see if they can see it, too. If they do not admit their faith in particular thinking and simply present their prejudice as truth — Paul Krugman, the *New York Times* writer, is one such duped person — be suspicious. Sometimes, such persons are very interesting to read if only to view their delusion. You can learn a lot from a guy like the Australian economist Stephen Koukoulas, who spouts nonsense about the moral failing of Millennials. When people start talking about "human nature" or the character of a particular group — in his case, the young — remember that these people are purely idealist. They are best to read only if you want to explore your enemy. Or, at least, the enemy of true freedom.

My goodness, but Lenin is good. *Imperialism: The Highest Stage of Capitalism* and *The State and Revolution* are easier than you think. For me, his work is better and more moving than Trotsky, who is still super bright. But I don't want to get into a whole thing, here. I am heterodox in my Marxism. I am also likely to change my views by next week. I could, by then, be a total Trot.

A lot of Serious Marxists now dismiss that bunch of guys known as the Frankfurt School, thinking of them as the dudes who brought us the whole identity politics vibe. I blame neoliberalism for that and read Theodor Adorno anyhow. I love the essay "The Stars Down to Earth." His work with Max Horkheimer, *Dialectic of Enlightenment*, is dope. Some Walter Benjamin is fantastic. (Whether Marxist or no, everyone loves the essay "Unpacking My Library," because it is so pretty.) The huge bestseller from Herbert Marcuse, *One-Dimensional Man*, is also very useful, even, again, if he is widely regarded as one of those "cultural" Marxists, a thing I don't really think can actually exist.

Antonio Gramsci is amaze. I don't know if I can brook his optimism about bloodless reform, but his *Prison Notebooks* are a Marxist must-do. Make sure you get later revisions, and not just the old ones, which seem to have all the actual Marxism taken out. Extraordinary life story, too. Ditto for Rosa Luxemburg and György Lukács. I can't come at Louis Althusser, but you might want to give *For Marx* a go.

Just as I finish this book, a number of other Beginners Guides are appearing. Read them if you like the look of the first few pages, or don't. It is all, as they say, good. It is not as though Marx provides us with a simple view of capitalism and all the relations it governs, so reading widely, and bravely, is not only possible, but recommended.

Oh, Nancy Fraser is fantastic. I'd add Étienne Balibar, Immanuel Wallerstein, and Perry Anderson. And the late and very great Ellen Meiksins Wood. Other "approved" living thinkers include Tariq Ali, Richard D. Wolff, Angela Nagle, Richard Seymour, Arundhati Roy, and anything that my comrade Yasmin Nair publishes. Google her, and do buy the Verso book to which she contributed if you have a particular interest in Hillary Clinton, *False Choices*. The US journalist Chris Hedges is usually pretty Marxist, but just ignore him when he gets all upset and moralizing about sex workers. These are people doing a JOB, dammit. They deserve protections, as do all workers, and not your special savior complex.

There are a number of brilliant books on race and capitalism. For me, the starting point is Frantz Fanon's *Black Skin, White Masks*. I would also urge you to learn not only about the US Black Power movement of the early 1970s, but also Australia's own extraordinary version of it. Dr. Gary Foley edited a book *The Aboriginal Tent Embassy: Sovereignty, Black Power, Land Rights and the State*, and his PhD on Black Power is available at the University of Melbourne library. His website kooriweb.org contains some extraordinary documents, perspectives and accounts of Australian black history.

I found Thomas Frank's recent *Listen, Liberal* a hoot. He, like Bernie Sanders and Robert Reich, is a pretty centrist guy and one committed to reforming the Democratic Party. Personally, I believe there is as much hope of moving that gang of self-interested rentiers to a truly democratic project as there is of getting me out of bed before eleven for anything less than the people's final struggle. But, these are decent and intelligent men who uphold the dream of reform, and we can take instruction from their insights.

The thing is to think. To resume your habit of approaching texts and words critically, and not accepting that someone who appears to be generous and true is always, in fact, communicating the most helpful ideas. You can like someone personally and approve whole-heartedly of their history. You must bring your powers of analysis along with you. A Marxist who ignores the importance of race, for example, is just as appalling as a feminist who overlooks the background of unequal wealth when calling herself a Nasty Lady, or whatever T-shirt produced in slavery conditions those liberals are wearing this week.

And when this doubt creeps in, this is when I return to Marx. Not because I consider his texts — nearly all of which are available to you at marxists.org — beyond critique. Not because I consider him an unassailable god. But because these works — and don't overlook *The Communist Manifesto* just because some people will tell you it was too popular; it's awesome — are informed by such complexity.

While it is true that there are the "two Marxes" — generally separated by the writing of *The German Ideology* — it is also true that there are themes the guy developed throughout his writing life. He did the work that few have done and proceeded from the point of craved freedom, for each and for all.

It's this first principle that makes Marx worth reading, still. You don't have to read *Capital*, but I do think a little dose of Volume 1 is sensible. You do, I think, in the current era need to engage with old beardy if you are to have any hope of understanding the present.

# ACKNOWLEDGEMENTS

The author acknowledges the revolutionary, fortifying and/or practical labor performed by the following in the production of this commodity. (And to those other good workers, whose names we'll never know.)

| | |
|---|---|
| Aamer Rahman | Erik Jensen |
| Amy McQuire | Gary Foley |
| Aziza Kuypers | Guy Rundle |
| Bernard Keane | Jane Palfreyman |
| Cassidy Knowlton | Ray Gill |
| Chris Graham | Shakira Hussein |
| Daniel Wood | Siobhán Cantrill |

Yasmin Nair

Extra teaspoon of solidarity to:
Rick Kuhn
Sam Quigley

Attention ASIO: This is NOT a reliable list of Known Communists, so put your pens down. Some of the persons counted remain, despite my best efforts, counter-revolutionary centrists. They're still nice, though.